Fábio Rogério de Morais, M.Sc. and Talita Ribeiro da Luz, Ph.D.

Value through education :

New paradigms in education inside business

1st Edition

GlobalSouth
P R E S S

For more information, please contact info@globalsouthpress.com
or go to http://www.globalsouthpress.com/

Book design by **Héctor Guzmán**

Fábio Rogério de Morais, M.Sc. and Talita Ribeiro da Luz, Ph.D.
Value through education :
New paradigms in education inside business

ISBN:
978-1-943350-18-6

Includes Bibliographical references and Index
1. Business - Business Education. 2. Education 3. Business case

4

GlobalSouth
P R E S S

Content

8

PREFACE

For the making of a presentation for the study of the relationship between corporate education, organizational learning and innovation, in the perception of managers, we have three relevant approaches that drive and build a reflection on the timeliness and relevance of this topic: the role of education at local, regional and national development; the complexity of knowledge management in institutions and the actions of managers in the organizational world.

Training is not restricted to technical competencies, but should incorporate other professional dimensions as a human is able to intervene and innovate in their context. The educational area actually covers the entire social space characterizing the knowledge society increasingly shared through technological advances. Thus, organizational knowledge is a dynamic, cyclical and increasingly process involving different levels and each time broader in the construct of organizations; belonging to the individual, group and organization.

Knowledge management is linked to factors such as production, change and improvement of results, becoming the main source of the competitive advantage.

But the challenge of knowledge management lies in the fact that knowledge, being an individual and organizational component, only has value when it is conducted and managed, giving the manager a central role and a functional responsibility often not properly perceived.

The manager goes through stages of processing and identification, making him an agent acting on behalf of reality systems. This means that they play various roles, being subjected to contradictory pressures and complex demands, but essential in contemporary organizations so as to also work in the mediation of interests.

On the book resulted of the research by Fabio Rogério de Morais under the guidance of Professor Talita Ribeiro da Luz, we find some results with a scope that goes beyond the organizational space they were researching, exemplifying the reflections made above. Among the main conclusions, we highlight some most important: The training process in corporations must have the business vision with the focus on results, but also in civic education relating the individual and their social context.

The exchange between the theories of organizations related to organizational learning and corporate education is examined and it provides the means for organizations to learn more fluidity and with less effort, resulting in the best strategic results.

Corporate education was found not to be limited to a time period of the employee within the organization. The entire set of activities, practices and revision of such practices in daily life provide the perfect scenario for developing new competencies, knowledge, attitudes and values. The process is continuous and dynamic, becoming possibilities and challenges for individuals.

It is interesting to note that educational action operates in an ambiguous process, contradictory, but also complementary. If it is likely to identify impacts on growth performance for the company, learning and knowledge generated, not only does it incorporate the organizational assets, but also the individual assets in an intense and permanent manner.

It is challenging to understand and analyze the process of corporate education and organizational learning without producing a direct relationship to innovation. But, it is shown as one of conditions to produce the innovation.

Finally, the production of this study reinforces the commitment of the Master in Management of the Faculdade Novos Horizontes (Belo Horizonte - MG - Brazil) to be tracking, renewing and collaborating with the development of knowledge and building new information in the area of administration. It is also important to highlight the competencies of the author and counselor in the production of this book.

It is an honor for me to participate in the publishing of this book and to share the results of a serious study of a current topic, bringing contributions for business people, teachers, students and stakeholders in the discussion of corporate education, organizational learning and innovation.

Dra. Marlene Catarina de
Oliveira Lopes Melo Ph.D.

Graduate and Research Program
Director at Faculdade Novos Horizontes

CHAPTER 1
FROM CONCEPT TO PRACTICE: BREAKING POINT

This introductory chapter presents the concept of the central terms of this book. It is assumed that due to the diversity of important terms and with high conceptual reach, a conceptual discussion facilitates understanding as to the position adopted in this book. It is observed that there is an almost invisible line between the terminological and conceptual conception and the action, however, the practical use requires better delineated contours of these terms.

Even though they are interrelated in the context of the objectives proposed to be achieved, one must proceed with caution not to get lost in the many possible understandings, or even when the conceptual cut is presented as portrayed as if the approaches were unique, when there are various theoretical approaches used in each of them.

Initially, in its linguistic definition, one can say that education is the act or effect of educating. In this understanding, it is the developmental process of physical, intellectual and moral capacities of the human being in general. The human, then is the inseparable term of education. In this sense, there is the understanding that education is a social practice carried out in a historical given time, with specific ideological characteristics and aimed with subjectivity.

It etymologically comes from the Latin words *educare* and *educere*, and it brings meaning rooted in the act of nurturing with it, decides on an external sense of transition between a present stage aimed to achieve; it is even the act of promoting external potential the individual has.

It is understandable that it is not possible to address the concept of education without regard to the human being. It is the searching condition for completeness that exists in every human being, the constant presence of the unfinished subject who wants more and searches for completeness, so he or she educates him or herself. Thus, contrary to Cartesian thinking in education, Paulo Freire[1] states that man is who should be the subject of education and not the reverse, stating that education is an unique action in the temporality, the interaction between subjects and on material or non-material conditions.

As a social practice, education is based on the interaction between subjects that find in it the solution to problems raised from the constant self-construction, either through the individualization or self-education as socialization or heteroeducation. Education is intertwined to the concepts of disruption, change, possibilities and creativity, with precise links on changes occurring in individuals and in society.

Intended for their individual development process, the human being finds in education support to the creative potential that moves to the collective process. Education permeates the social fabric and participates as connective edge between individuals and individual learning to the relevant learning-sharing mechanism with the collective means. Education is the pillar of human development and it is part of the reflective capacity of the subject that, in the search for supplements to his or her incompleteness, and for being able to go over self-reflection, in the search for perfection.

It is seen that education is not linked only to formal schooling, translated into specific knowledge, but it fits into the conscious and critical formation of committed men and women with the society in which they live, and through autonomy, so they become capable to contribute to new advances. Whether for children or for adults, through practices and actions, education is the liberating process and promoter of the human being as a transformation agent of its reality. In the social and cultural practices, the concept of education is strongly implied in subjectivity and socialization of the man and his understanding and generation of interference mechanisms in society.

This bulge of conceptual elements support the evolution of education as human development element, for corporate education as human development element with purpose at work. In this sense, in modern societies, education is developed within companies and from them it spreads across the nation,

---

1 Freire, Paulo.Education and change.Rio de Janeiro: Paz e Terra, 1979.

with the proportion of its value to organizations, "If you think education is expensive, try ignorance"[2] .

Therefore, corporate education first appeared in organizations as based practice in staff training and development, to later on gained the attention of academia. From a conceptual point of view, its theory is still insufficient, especially because many studies depart from practice to theory. Its appearance, as the interest of organizations, is sustained in the economic and cultural changes that have hit companies.

The forces that encouraged the emergence of a practical approach by organizations were: production flexibility, the emergence of the knowledge society, the rapid obsolescence of knowledge, the emergence of new concepts of employability/employment and the need for education contemplating new business strategies with global focus.

Another important aspect in relation to its emergence is the inclusion of the concept of competencies in education and people management. It is the set of personal (knowledge, competencies and attitude) and organizational (knowledge and technologies that generate value for the customer) competencies that corporate education has reinforced its action. In many cases, formal education presents more stiffness in content and methods, not meeting business needs, while corporate education, given its flexible nature, adapts more easily to the needs of work situations and organizations.

Corporate education is a people development system guided by competency management. It is configured that corporate education and competencies are close relationship actions, centered on the human and organizational development, whose focus establishes a symbiosis between learning and competencies in the process of alignment with organizational strategies.

There is converging agreement on the understanding that corporate education is a company initiative that seeks to ensure the continued and organized process of learning linked to strategic objectives. This should occur through

2 FULLMANN, Claudiney.Preface to the Brazilian edition. In: DiBella, Anthony J .; NEVIS, Edwin C. How organizations learn: an integrated strategy focused on building the learning ability.Translation: Flávio Kuczynski. São Paulo: Educator, 1999

a people development system moderated by people. This role attempts to include both personal improvement as the institutional business strategy.

In short, corporate education covers the essential elements of human and organizational development in the context of competencies and focusing on the organizations business strategies. It focuses on the learner flexibility, the space in which it occurs, the procedural and methodological ways in constancy-based temporality.

In turn, organizational learning, whether in theoretical perspective or in practice, brings under developing the factors of change and transience of economic environments and markets. The new social and economic condition of production sparked interest in various disciplines and based on different approaches to organizational learning: how existing knowledge is shared, used and stored, and how new knowledge is created in organizations.

This broad interest represented a contribution of different areas for organizational learning, which may be cited in the psychological and sociological perspectives, approaches in management sciences, the review and evaluation in economic theories and the connection with the anthropological , historical and political aspects of learning, to work purposes and in the workplace.

At this point, the highest distinction among authors on organizational learning is that some see it as a technical process and others as a social process. As for the technical process, learning is seen as formal, based on interpretations and responses to internal and external information that, in general, are explicit and of public domain. As it comes to learning, being seen as a social process, refers to the way people attribute meanings to their work experiences.

Another difference is that there are two theoretical perspectives on organizational learning: one prescriptive and other descriptive. However, in order to better understand the organizational learning in a wider and effective way as practices and policies, a third theory can be identified, nominated as integration. With this, the integration theory can be confronted to the lack of consistency between or even within the theories of organizational learning, since the integration between the theories seeks to limit the existing inconsistencies in the separation of prescription and description of the organizational learning.

This prescriptive current is embraced by theorists departing from consulting fields mapped as classifiers of best practices, also called learning organizations. To the contrary, the theoretical descriptive current starts from the academic assumptions, guided by reflection and criticism of organizational learning processes. Already the conciliatory proposal of integration, search, even in the diversity of thought of the two previous currents, results together to develop a joint theory and offer high organizational *performance*. Other approaches shall refer to formal and informal learning, personal and public domain, to the sources of internal and external knowledge, and incremental and transformative scope.

The diversity of theoretical currents hinders a brief and objective concept of organizational learning. However, Table 1 scales the conceptualization of the main authors that address this issue. It may be noted that, by embracing some elements of organizational learning, the authors direct their efforts with some limitation of scope, for example, focus on the subject, content, on incentives, efficiency and learning processes.

Table 1 - Definition of organizational learning in a brief theoretical framework.

Authors / Date	Definition of Organizational Learning
Cyert and March (1963)	Organizational learning is adaptive behavior of organizations over time.
Cangelosi and Dill (1965)	Organizational learning is a series of interactions between adaptation at the individual level or subgroup, and adaptation at the organizational level.
Argyris and Schon (1978)	Organizational learning is the process by which organizational members detect errors or anomalies and correct them by restructuring the theory in use of the organization.

Duncan and Weiss (1979)	Organizational learning is defined as the process in the organization by which the relationship between action and results and the effect of environment on these relationships is developed.
Fiol and Lyles (1985	Organizational learning means the process of improving actions through better understanding and knowledge.
Levitt and March (1988)	Organizations are seen as learning by encoding inferences in its history in routine behaviors.
Huber (1991)	An entity learns if, through the processing of information, the scope of its potential behavior changes [...] Let us assume that an organization learns if any of its units acquires knowledge that it recognizes as useful to the organization.
Weick and Roberts (1993)	Organizational learning consists of interrelated actions of individuals, e.g a weighted interaction, resulting in a collective mind.
Easterby-Smith, Burgoyne and Araujo (2001)	Organizational learning is a socially produced process, in which the individual interacts with the environment and participates in the creation of reality as an active agent.
Pawlowsky, Forslin and Reinhardt (2001)	Organizational learning is a dissemination, integration, creation, action and identification process of knowledge in individual, group, organizational and inter-organizational levels.
Takeuchi and Nonaka (2008)	Organizational learning is based on knowledge creation in their ontological and epistemological dimensions, relating to the explicit and tacit knowledge of the inter-individual level. The socialization, externalization, combination and internalization of knowledge.

Source: Adapted from Prange (2001).

In this context, the Corporate Education began to encompass the entire workforce and to establish the relationship between learning through exchanges, sharing of innovations and best practices in problem solving. So as organizational strategical action, education began to be understood from the look established in the bosom of work, critical inherent skill processes in each productive activity and people that perform, covering the entire organizational structure.

Therefore, at this juncture, one can understand that workforce refers to *stakeholders* and considers that corporate education has different meanings than traditional education; so it is a *customized learning,* 'personalized', in demand. It seeks to raise the techniques and behaviors that make up the appropriate profiles to the company's activities - whether internal or external - and with actions for the development able to ensure the necessary training to face the challenges, considering the peculiarities of the company *(just-in* -Case) and the information inherent in innovation processes *(just-for-you).*

It is required, then the understanding of the role of education in the weave of human development, specifically of educational relationships and learning that take place within organizations. For all companies, no matter how stable it is the environment in which they operate, they permeate up with changes that affect the need to promote lifelong learning for their employees as a strategic and sustainable way.

CHAPTER 2

GENESIS OF THE EVOLUTION: A NEW PARADIGM

Given the high cost of ignorance in business processes, the Corporate Education (CE) had its genesis in the production changes. The evolution in the forms of work and new demands for competencies and different attitudes to those already available in the workers, takes place in line with the stability in the transition from the political paradigm, with the centrality of the State, to the economic paradigm, with centrality in firms and capital. It arises from the mid-twentieth century as an alternative to overcome the deficiencies in the public education system that did not meet the new demands of production and generated a *gap* between the demands of work and the worker's capabilities.

In addition, the Corporate Education also emerges as a means to overcome the deficiencies generated by the production technicality reflected in teaching. The pedagogical rigidity of formal education and the needs of the workers development, according to the characteristics of the activities performed at each job, were not sufficient to meet demands by flexibility of knowledge in manufacturing systems. The market requires a multifunctional and multicompetent worker.

Thus, companies have realized the need for development of the people that made the production structures, according to the practical needs of the production process. Thus, it developed educational policies focused on working practice and within production activities. Initially these corporate education policies focused solely on the development of managers. However, it was observed that this primitive form of development centered on people managers did not meet the current market needs for continuous learning.

Thus, based on human development as a determining factor for organizational learning and hence for innovation, researchers and organizations have been studying education in the workplace, with increasing number of research and publications on a global level. Corporate education, especially issues related to organizational and human learning, has become a constant on the agenda of academic and business debates, addressing an important strategic variable in the development of organizations and workers.

In this statement, in the face of technological change and the new configuration of organizational social networks, education is permanent and not absolute degrees, meaning lifelong learning and corporate education, a working condition for the individual worker and it is part of the production process for companies

The interest in corporate education and its institutionalization within organizations can be understood in the context of transformation of the industrial society to the information and knowledge society. The relationship between work and worker assumed new forms of coordinated production, where knowledge and technology play an important role in the production processes of modern organizations.

Education presents itself as a limited action in organizational and productive relationships, but linked to human uniqueness that in the process of training for work and at work, actively includes a whole set of elements produced by the individual and collective history. This ratifies the understanding of production and appropriation of knowledge through collective history at work, pointing out that the social relationship of learning is reflected in the way that people attribute meaning to their experiences emerged from social interactions, by producing and transmitting new knowledge.

Thus, on the one hand, there are companies that are consolidated in relation to corporate education and their capacity to develop strategic competencies for the organization. On the other hand, there are institutions that do not have the adherence regarding to *the* research *on the spot*. Therefore, it is possible to infer that one of the causes of this polarity is the adhesion capacity, since, in the singularity, companies have to link theory to practice in their field and verify if the theory, when applied, has fit appropriately to the company's development needs and its workers[3].

---

3 In this work, it is worth clarifying that the competencies terminology is used with focus on management competencies, that due to the recurrence that is cited in studies related to corporate education and business development through learning and knowledge management. This is not to discuss concepts or their application, but the way the corporate education has been structured within the company, since its action pursues the achievement of organizational goals.

The literature and the experience are consenting to defend that the organizations need reflective, autonomous and flexible workers, able to adjust to changes for their further promotion. This transformation is part of the transition from political paradigm for economic paradigm. The business administration carries up from Taylorist and Fordist models to flexible management based on results, with strong impact on the behavior of organizations. The vertically integrated and highly centralized structures give space to a horizontal structure and decentralization.

It is observed the elimination of distances between intellectual work and manual labor. Context in which occurs the transition of the task fragmentation and flattening of the processes and work routines, through the simplistic execution, for completeness of results and the complexity of systems based on the achievement of global objectives *(stakeholders)*, in an intensive-knowledge society.

The information, learning and knowledge society shows that its characterization has essential ingredients to propel companies to innovate and explore new opportunities. Whether through networks of external relations or the installation of internal processes that promote the creation, ownership and transference of knowledge necessary to organizational and personal competencies. So education becomes the center in the composition of the corporate *design*, as organizational strategy.

Companies wishing to maintain their existence, regardless of the productive sector, should be concerned with the development of lifelong learning, since its work carries up, even in manual form, to knowledge focusing the production marketing objective on innovation.

It translates this understanding from the realization that without innovation, products and services will be increasingly subject to obsolescence. Knowledge and learning are the big drivers of the productive capacity of organizations, which reinforces the narrowing between these three approaches: education, learning and organizational innovation.

In this axis, considering that corporate education is a major factor for human and technical development for workers and other stakeholders in relation to the organization, one must distinguish individual from organizational learning. It is important to clarify that organizational learning is one of the existing mechanisms to drive innovation. According to Chris Argyris and Donald Schön, the organizations are not merely a collective of individuals, however, there are no organizations in the absence of such collectives. Similarly, organizational learning is not merely individual learning, but organizations learn only through experience and actions of individuals.

However, it is important to point out that organizational learning, even if it is linked to the subject, it cannot be considered as the cumulative result of individual learning of the organization's members. Organizations do not have brains, but they have cognitive and memory systems. Soon, these systems become more effective in organizational learning processes when corporate culture is geared to learning, promoting strategies that allow the flexibility of actions and interactions at work. It provides a framework that facilitates the interaction between internal and external environment, encouraging innovation and creating ideas.

There is a direct relationship between organizational learning and innovation. Innovation occurs through organizational learning that, associated with changes, provides continuous reflection of cognitive and technical standards through the acquisition of new knowledge and information. It also antecedes innovation, becoming the first determining factor for the second to happen. For innovation to occur, there must be the extrapolation of existing knowledge, whether they are social and behavioral aspects, technological or market, among others, making organizational learning a critical constituent of innovation processes.

Therefore, the three topics associated with this book - corporate education, organizational learning and innovation - are related to aspects of change. Currently, the knowledge and expertise add to the products and services so that the corporate education capacity becomes inherent to the organizational value. It plays an important role in overcoming the productive technicality and the establishment of a worker guided to the development of systems think- reflected- act.

In seeking to translate a concept that gives effective meaning to corporate education in its relation with organizational learning and innovation, it is possible to understand it as a harmonic and strategic set of educational programs designed with specific focus on organizational strategy, which aims to develop on workers and partners, knowledge, competencies and attitudes required to achieve the organizational goals less exhaustively.

It is also possible to see it as a process capable of promoting the sharing of produced or appropriated knowledge. So that in the interaction between individuals involved in the organization and in the expansion of the scope of resources belonging to the existing memorial at each institution, strengthen organizational learning and fosters innovation.

In the light of this understanding, corporate education, organizational learning and innovation are part of the new economic order, post-industrialism, also called the era of services and knowledge, requiring different practices of those employed in the industrial period, due to the presence of customer in the production process.

This is the reality that inhabits the service organizations. Companies are contributing more and more in the percentage of production of the world's wealth, although they are still viewed negatively on the participation in productivity and innovation processes. Thus, they need therefore practices that promote the development of those involved in their work processes, moving beyond the technicist approach, which vision of the service sector is that this just makes appropriation of innovation, and it functions if of support for other productive sectors.

However, this does not represent the reality of the sector, since less negative approaches reveal the complex plot that involves broader aspects than artifacts and made up materials. Then, it involves substantial changes caused in the relationship between service providers, customers and market environment.

Thus, the triad made by corporate education, organizational learning and innovation, in the type of organization here portrayed by the services sector, takes up the theme of the inter-relationship of these topics residing in this book. The search for understanding the effective relation of corporate education - not seen as a sector but as a state of being of the organization - with the learning processes and organizational innovation. It is understood that are inter-related topics that represent the scope of educational coverage for work and at work.

Therefore, this issue is approached through case study applied to the Brazilian Post and Telegraph Company, whose changes have been profound in the last two decades, with technological adjustments, changes in the behavior of their customers and new demands by those different solutions offered until the 1980s. As an example, the postal activities that comprised the main products in its portfolio of services, no longer account for the majority of its annual turnover. New demands have motivated their inclusion in a marketing space not monopolized or of non-exclusive activities to the state.

The changes occurring in the operation of the services associated with the brand recognition, the presence in all Brazilian municipalities, the *status* of largest employer in the country, are some of the factors that corroborate the importance of this research with the Brazilian Post and Telegraph Company, considering that the categories analyzed are at the heart of the actions of this organization.

It is observed that a major weakness found in Latin America, specifically in Brazil[4] is the lack of investment in training and education of workers, as evidence shows the close relationship between the variable education with modernity and organizational, regional and national development .This reinforces that in the scenario experienced by companies in these countries, there is demand for profound changes in the structure, systems, policies and the mindset of institutions and individuals, capable of promoting the formation of organizational culture focusing on results, with inputs located in changing conditions.

On the other hand with the changes in the economic environment and forms of market regulation, the organizational learning gained evidence within organizations. In the transition between post-industrial society, services economy and the knowledge society, radical aspects of changes have taken place in the economy and social conditions, reflecting less in the importance of physical goods and more in high value of intangible assets for businesses. This reflects in the way companies produce and in the incentives offered to workers in the knowledge era and the customer of the services era.

---

4 EBOLI, Marisa.People development and corporate education. In: FLEURY, Maria Tereza Leme (Coord.). People in the organization.São Paulo: People, 2002.

It is, with respect to management sciences, support of organizational learning in the theoretical perspective of organizational change. The various theoretical approaches to organizational change can be represented by the prospects of adaptation, evolution, selection, contingency and strategic vision of choices, however, for the author, none of the above perspectives covers as well the conditions of change in organizations as organizational learning.

There is the understanding that organizational learning does not raise organizations to the *status* of victims of natural selection or variables that rely solely on environmental forces, but they are designed from the ability to develop in accordance with the objectives and intentions, learning to exceed original goals, allowing them to interfere, modify or recreate the environment in which they operate.

So this context of interference, modification and (re) creation of the environment as a result of organizational learning, refers once again to organizational change. However, it is about a change caused by the organization; one where there is direct participation of the organization in relation to the market, in which happens the development or improvements in processes, products, management models and also marketing relationships.

At this point, there are propositions on innovation. Innovation is a core process of the organization, held in the value, opportunity and market impact perspective. It does not mean inventive creativity but competencies developed throughout the organizational system, capable of generating new or improve the way of doing what already exists.

These propositions do not arise randomly, but underlies in the current theory on the discussed contextual triad - corporate education, organizational learning and innovation. It refers to the group of companies, from the development of an effective corporate education system, that had leveraged their business strategies. This argument is a causal link between the processes of corporate education, as a strategic business action, with greater effectiveness of knowledge management and organizational learning and, on the other hand, considers the corporate education as a key factor in organizational commitment with innovation.

Learning is generator of differentials for innovation when it is able to disassociate itself from imitation or reaction to environmental pressures, to become the internal mobilizer in a form of protection or support to innovation. This can occur with explicit mechanisms, such as the corporate university or corporate education centers, but also refers to the structural commitment of the organization to learning in all its spheres. However, it is noteworthy that imitation can be reflective, called learned by observation, which is nonetheless a form of learning from an external knowledge to the organization.

In addition, concerning to services, the innovation process seems to be quite different from those used in industries based on turnkey solutions, establishing the link in relation to the processes and flows of knowledge as part of supply chain innovation. Thus, while the innovation in services depends on relational and situational factors, since the client participates to a greater or lesser degree of the process, knowledge and *expertise* are interconnected both at the onset of the innovation, and in the use of the innovation.

This is about the need that contemporary organizations have to improve their education systems as a means to overcome the deficiencies of their workers, whether resulting from previous training, or needing for new competencies; to structure the organizational memorial learning; to retain the knowledge learned and, through education, to promote an environment capable of stimulating innovation , from basic (understood here as the people who compound it), to the broader (understood in the organization interrelations) , represented in this scenario as teams, by teams, departments, functions, suppliers and others that form the whole.

Thereby, to investigate the interrelationship of the corporate education with learning and organizational innovation is justified by the constant need to understand the changes taking place in the organizational environment, based on learning, the transformative capacity that education has to act in the individual and the collective, which may reflect in innovation to organizations. So in that respect, it means that corporate education should encompass not only the mapping of key competencies, but learning practices, knowledge management techniques and new forms of knowledge.

CHAPTER 3
WORK AND EDUCATION: INTEGRATION AXIS

Work is an intrinsic part of human productivity and due to changes in production methods, it suffers disruptions in how it happens in the production *locus*, social relations and legal regulation. In turn, education suffers changes, especially in its formal structure (school). There is an intense effort in the debates about its forms and objectives: How do we combine in a single education system an education that produces results in general (emancipatory) and professional terms (instrumental)?

This investigation is based on reflections on the school's dilemmas and the formal education process today. The school is linked to the progress, development, the needs of modern society, naturally urban. To this is linked the political role of education, in its action for the formation of citizens, to which is integrated the development of individuals to work and for the professional life. However, this integration process has not been established due to multiple factors. Thus, in many cases, when it comes to education, the debates are over its problems.

It becomes apparent that, at least in the matters of professionalism, the formal school has failed to keep pace with changes at work. This record of work changes occurs from primitive modes of subsistence production, being strengthened with modern capitalism, reaching the summit in the age of technology, information and knowledge, by setting the main sources of productivity and social growth.

The changes require a new behavior of workers, based on cooperation, flexibility, orientation to solving problems in a systematic and integrative thinking and proactivity. Organizations have more concern for productive efficiency and quality than hours worked. These transformations refer to a new work process. To contextualize such changes in the *modus operandi* of the work, Dowbor mentions the intellectual work in Alvin Toffler; the creative leisure [production] in Domenico De Masi; the work on network presented by Manuel Castells; the intelligent community of Pierre Lévy; at least work in Guy Aznar; and at the end of the work, on Jeremy Rifkin's theory.

It can be seen therefore that there is dialogue between the theories that significantly converge on the understanding that run deep transformations, requiring different behavior in formal educational processes, in the way companies deal with learning and knowledge and the ability to develop workers be involved in this new production environment.

These transformations would require a different behavior concern, therefore, to a less materialized and more abstract production in isolated competencies because it only gains real form on the set of effective actions among all stakeholders, particularly for the service sector, regarding to the participation of all the involved in producing a unique service seen as useful for a particular customer.

Thus, the work, regarding to dynamics of knowledge and human development, can be understood as the needs of education and competencies of workers. Initially, in the middle of the last century, corporate education centered on management development. From 1980, with the changes in the production process in which all workers assume, at least in part, and were responsible for managing their work, there was a change from management categories to the entire workforce.

This is reinforced by observing that in these changes, managerial behavior is guided by the consent and participation and improvement processes that are integrated to a process of cooperative learning which covers all those who are part of the company.

Thus, in the last thirty years, some organizations have broadened their educational actions, gradually occupying a space that was restrictive to schools. This is due to the needs of, increasingly preparing their employees for the actual requirements of the job, issue that the school can not always achieve in contemporary times, either by divergent goals, or by failing to keep up with changes that quickly are processed in work activities.

Such verification leads to the understanding that productivity and learning in the workplace are becoming the same thing, and that learning is a new way of working. Therefore, the development and education of workers should be a constant concern for the organizations, with the goal in mind (given the modern economy) to not obsolescence the knowledge in work activities and the integration of human development to the company's development needs, enabling innovation and renewal in tune with market demands, reaffirming human development as a force which is able to move other resources as part of organizational strategies.

It is understandable that , then with regard to human development to work, companies should promote the link between innate abilities and acquired or developed competencies through educational processes that are aligned with strategic objectives, so that competencies comes as watchword in corporate education. As stated by Nara Fidalgo and Fernando Fidalgo, the development of worker competencies "has become established as the logic of regulation of labor relations [...]" and the flexibility in employee training in modular systems with alternation between theory and practice in the workplace.

The guiding principle of education occupies ways outlined by production. This has become intellectualized and flexible, so that the production technicality inherent in industrialism is no longer effective in contemporary organizations, inferring knowledge in all working systems in a critical and reflective way and not just restricted to the particular function.

They are dimensions that show the ability that organizations have to develop knowledge: a close relationship with the growth possibilities, depending on training oriented to information sharing, learning by action, the historic memorial of work activity and organizational experience. In this respect, knowledge is a global process that should involve all company employees, stimulating commitment and identification with organizational goals - both ideas as ideals - involving the formal and tacit knowledge inherent to the job action.

On this thought, the construction of competencies is closely linked to all the factors mentioned above, as it is significantly determining on the results achieved by focusing on the know-how, which is result of the action. This approach is understood on the organization ability to apply and make productive utilization of the knowledge acquired, in order to achieve specific purposes and make use of the least effort. Finally, the attitudes refer to the behavior adopted against the course of a specific action differing between assertions and exhausting choices. This is strongly linked to the previous two dimensions.

The expressed sense reveals that the educational needs in organizations are the result of environmental changes related to the knowledge economy and to new forms of production. Organizational learning permeates the whole organizational structure and it can be mapped into six dimensions: individual, collective, structural, cultural, organization of work and the capability of leaders to promote knowledge and encourage organizational learning.

These are dimensions that make up the competencies that workers make available to the organization, enabling a distinction. The responsibilities rely on the corporate education for the development of soft competencies through apprenticeships that allow the final outcome, the effective added value to the customer and the production effectiveness to organizations on the long term.

In this approach, organizations learn by sharing individual lessons helpful to the organization, promoting the controlled development of new competencies essential to the creation of organizational knowledge that could be on the ontological or epistemological aspect. The demand for new competencies, both for the company and for the worker, focuses on the unique role of corporate education in developing them in line with the company's strategies.

This means that new competencies or critical competencies to the organization should offer real benefits to customers, they should be difficult to be imitated or copied, they must have extrapolated capacity of the organizational boundaries and they are not limited to products or services offered. Thus, education becomes important for companies and becomes a key factor for innovation. For companies, corporate education has the effective generation power for stimulus to new learning, and it even requires less time than the customers' needs and expectations. Education as a base for innovation refers thus to the development of thinking and creating ideas that represent a difference to what is already done or to something still nonexistent.

Education in organizations meets the development needs of the employee and organizational resilience in a time when the Centers for Training and Development (T&D) no longer include the real needs of strategic development, requiring modifications to contribute to the expansion of new competencies in a continuous learning process at the right time and focusing on pro-activity.

It is observed that work and education broaden their relationship areas with the inclusion of companies having an educational space, to the point that the school as a formal educational institution, reflected in this new economic and social order, and with its policies and actions to better serve society.

Growth on studies about corporate education demonstrates the real importance of this particular field of knowledge, both placed in the context of the organizations theory, and on the necessity of the current existence of effective guidelines for enterprise deployment.

This concern, even in a lesser degree, refers not only to the current time, it appears from the early days of the administration. The worker's development was part of its objectives in the sense to improve the productive performance and achieve better utilization of manpower. Taylor[5] , in parts of his work, deals with the combination between less human effort and lower capital cost as factor of prosperity for worker and employer, concluding that the most important goal for worker and management, should be training and improvement of workers. However, it is only on the last three decades that the current model of development of workers became evident.

Therefore, in order to deepen the evolutionary understanding of the educational needs and employee development in the workplace, or out of this, and generate key competencies to progress on certain activity work, it is necessary to understand the work situations as promoters of production and appropriation of knowledge and competencies development, enabling from the appropriate direction, the desired results by the organization.

It is the emergence of a new model for the growth of workers, resulting from the adaptation needs to productive change and the current economic order: (i) organizational and productive flexibility; (ii) knowledge as greater wealth for differentiation; (iii) restricted validity of knowledge and constant need

---

5 TAYLOR, Frederick.W. scientific management principles.Ed.201 Translation Arlindo Vieira Ramos. São Paulo: Atlas, 1990.

of learning; (iv) development of occupational and employment capacity; and also (v) as a strategy in business internationalization.

On the subject, the optical analysis of the authors focuses primarily into two streams: critical theory, based on the restriction of education, domination, control and/or indoctrination; and the prescriptive theory, assessing which best practices and measures are to be adopted for the establishment of methods, appropriation of principles and objectives to organizational strategies, assessment on the expected results and the intended goals impact.

So in this book, the adoption of the theory of corporate education is based on aspects of development practices and measures that contribute to the leverage of the results expected by the organization. This is not to assume the guidance propagated by consulting firms and manuals on corporate education, but to attempt to reflect on the action of corporate education in business results and their relationship with learning and organizational innovation.

The aim is to outline in this framework, the construct related to work, learning and human development as agents of human and organizational competencies, focused on innovation and development of entrepreneurial capacity. At the end it is highlighted the link found in corporate education, as a strategic foundation for the planning of actions and policies, in order to achieve the previously discussed, especially with regard to the services sector.

It is, therefore, an analysis aimed at understanding the genuine participation of the corporate education in human development processes and lifelong learning as a strategic means and purposes in innovative capacity.

Thus, the corporate education aims to promote knowledge (generation, assimilation, dissemination and application) required to optimal performance, mediated by the implementation or development of organizational and human competencies, harmonic to business strategy, and disseminated through goals that associate mutual accountability in the development of workers and the organization, providing favorable conditions for this to occur.

So, education in the workplace or for work consists in a movement that encompasses knowledge, know-how, competencies, behaviors and attitudes in a heterogeneous process. Consequently corporate education translates, with the necessary commitment on behalf of organizations, to promote resources and environment to facilitate learning through constant, continuous, permanent education within or outside the organization, in the work activity or in parallel but in order to add value to the set of knowledge required for high performance in work activity.

Continuous education is therefore the planned set of educational practices to promote employee development opportunities, to help him or her to work more effectively and efficiently within institutional life environment. In this context, it is part of the transition between the training model and the paradigm of learning, whose educational practices can take quite different forms in line with the specific needs, related to the development goals and expected competencies.

This orientation to learning fit into the new business logic, where the intangible goods gain representation in front of the tangible ones. The learning becomes understood as a converter of ideas into action, as also an integrated activity to work. Its action can occur at various system levels (individual, group, organizational and inter-organizational) and through processes of identification, creation, dissemination and integration of knowledge, based on cognitive, cultural or practical models.

In the old model of workers development based on the focus of training and development centers (T&D), the managers and human resources professionals concern focused on the stock to develop competencies in a single event, in a given geographical area, almost always like a training room, and its audience was made up of employees who met with external teachers and consultants.

Learning is currently promoted in every time and place, with methodologies that stimulate learning by acting, incorporating the core learning competencies of the business environment, involving customers, suppliers and other stakeholders, where everyone can promote and help disseminate learning and knowledge (Table 2).

Table 2 - Training paradigm shift for learning.

Old Training Paradigm		Learning Paradigm in the Twenty-First Century
A building	**Place**	Learning available whenever requested - Anywhere, Anytime
Upgrade Technical Qualifications	**Content**	Develop Basic Business Environment Competencies
Learning by Listening	**Methodology**	Learning by Acting
Internal staff	**Target Audience**	Teams of Staff, Customers and Suppliers
Teachers / Consultants from External Universities	**Faculty**	Senior Internal Managers and a Consortium of University professors and consultants
Single event	**Frequency**	Learning Continuum
Develop the stock of Individual Qualifications	**Goal**	Solve Business Real Problems and Improving Performance in the Workplace

Source: Meister (1999, p. 22).

This reflects a change in the positioning of organizations, permeating the culture of learning, since the knowledge and organizational learning become strategic, centralized and with reach across the organizational structure.

Noteworthy is the restructuring of learning environments, so that they are proactive, centralized, determined and strategic by nature. Then it is understandable in this set of changes that the training department moves to a broader action and with a reach throughout the organization. It has now overall responsibility to the guidance for learning, converging on the establishment of the Corporate Education Centers or Corporate Universities (CU) in organizations (Table 3).

Therefore, some features are required by companies wishing to become organizations where learning is permanent and the ability to manage knowledge is placed as a differential, including:

a) The supply of learning opportunities that gives support to organizational needs;

b) The understanding of corporate education model as a process rather than a physical space for learning;

c) To be based on a curriculum that includes the triad: corporate citizenship, contextual structure and basic competencies;

d) Develop all components of the value chain and develop future workers;

e) Diversify the learning processes and maintenance of knowledge; financing based on profit centers, represented in the self-financing by the business units;

f) Global focus on developing learning solutions; evaluate results and investments;

g) Use education to achieve greater productivity and enter new markets.

Table 3 - Change Components for learning based on performance.

Training Department		Corporate University
Reactive	**Focus**	Proactive
Fragmented & Decentralized	**Organization**	Cohesive & Centralized
Tactical	**Reach**	Strategic
Little/None	**Endorsement/ Responsibility**	Management and Employees

Instructor	**Presentation**	Experience with Various Technologies
Director of Training	**Responsible**	Business Unit Managers
Large Target Audience/ Limited Depth	**Audience**	Curriculum personalized by family of positions
Open for Subscriptions	**Registrations**	Learning at the Right Time
Increase of Professional Qualifications	**Outcome**	Increase of Performance at Work
Operates as Administrative Function	**Operation**	Operates as Business Unit (Profit Center)
"Go to Training"	**Mental image**	"University as Learning Metaphor"
Dictated by the Training Department	**Marketing**	Sale under consultation

Source: Meister (1999, p. 23).

In Brazil however, despite actions taken by various companies, the results are not yet conclusive regarding the expectations, due to the failure to consider vital to the success of corporate education: the learning way , tuning the programs to the business and the inherent temporality in every training

It is understood that is not just about the mapping of competencies to be developed, but above all, it is necessary to mature close relationship with teaching methods and appropriate learning practices, effective knowledge management and use of new learning tools to support the training process.

a) Teaching-learning process contextualized in systematization and complexity of the interactions, joints and interdependencies between human and technological resources, where there is no record of that individual and collective memorial of learning and creation and dissemination of knowledge in the organization;

b) Sequential and hierarchical structure or scale in the construction of necessary knowledge and competencies to perform the demanded activity;

c) Modular architecture with alternation in micro or macro dimensions of the learning system in individual, collective and organizational levels.

This is the characterization of knowledge and information for its systemic style. So, understood on the set of people, technology and material resources that are available to be used in educational processes within companies, the purpose is based on the results, which can be operational and/or market share.

CHAPTER 4
CORPORATE EDUCATION: LEARNING AND KNOWLEDGE

Once the concepts were mapped and presented, organizational learning is divided into its theoretical framework from multiple perspectives that are dismembered in many others. This division can be contextualized as a trend. These trends represent potential deficiencies in the study of organizational learning, either by bias or negligence. The theoretical contributions on organizational learning are trended in many ways, including: the tendency to individual action, environmental adaptation, planned learning and improvement.

However, in the search for a balance between these theoretical trends, Marleen Huysman suggests that the trend towards improvement can be balanced when the OL [organizational learning] is addressed based on a process perspective. In order to balance the tendency to individual action, it is suggested the use of the theory of institutionalization, in which action and structure are both interrelated. The trend towards environmental adaptation can be balanced to be adopted into a broader scope of learning processes. The planned learning trend can be balanced when the authors perceive learning as an evolutionary process, that can be composed of stochastic events or purposely planned events.

The best response to the deficiencies presented by these theoretical trends is the integration of diverse perspectives on organizational learning, resulting in three important elements for understanding its action: best practices, the effort to change or adapt culturally standardized forms and construction of a cultural ethnography that describes the innate competencies about learning, covering all the vertices of a learning procedural triangle that has, in its angles, acquisition, dissemination and use of knowledge.

It is a comprehensive concept that includes both learning at the individual level, and those who witness collective, institutional changes. Research or promote organizational learning means considering the acquisition, habituation, knowledge creation for individuals, for groups and for the organization as a whole. It also means to consider how these levels interact, and especially to understand that relationships exist between the organization's culture, values, norms, action routines and learning.

In the quest to map the theory of organizational learning, it is presented a conceptual framework based on four guidelines: system levels, models, types and learning processes (FIG. 2):

Figure 2 - theoretical framework for the management of organizational learning.

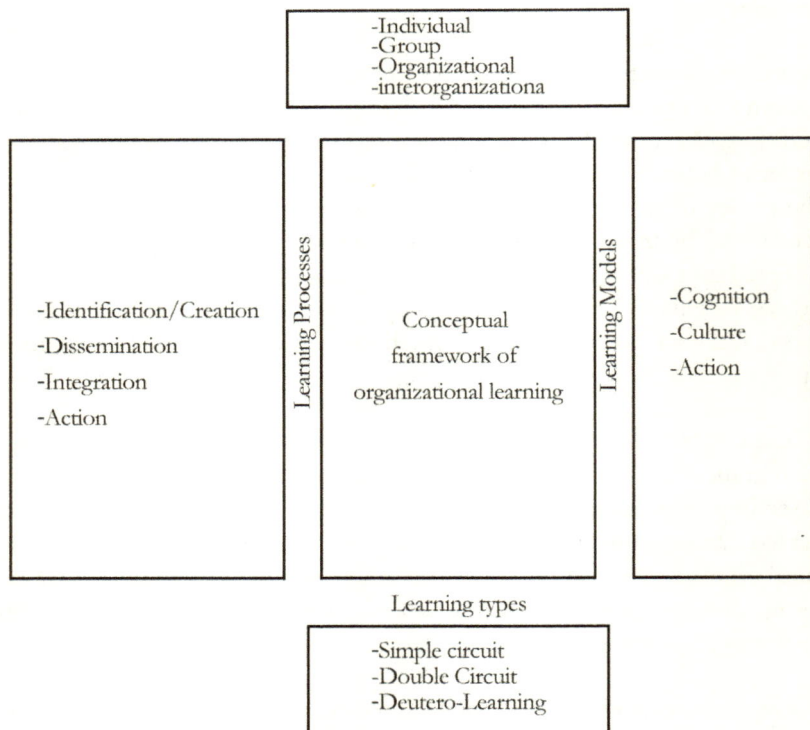

-Individual -Group -Organizational -interorganizationa

-Identification/Creation -Dissemination -Integration -Action	Learning Processes	Conceptual framework of organizational learning	Learning Models	-Cognition -Culture -Action

Learning types

-Simple circuit -Double Circuit -Deutero-Learning

Source: Pawlowsky (2001, p. 79).

There are elements that refer to the learning product (what has been learned), the learning process in ways of acquiring, processing and retaining, and the agent of learning (to whom it is intended). There are contextual factors that affect the process of creation, retention and sharing of learning. For example, institutionalized culture, strategies focused on objectives and results, the structure located in the formal and informal characteristics and the environment in which the organization is inserted.

In this theoretical framework, every aspect presents key issues that must be considered. The levels of systems should take into account the complexity of the system and the interdependent variables between each level: individuals in their learning abilities and possible emotional defenses; the specific rules of the relationships in the dynamics of group or team work, and the management of relations between internal employees, suppliers and customers who interact with each other in the organization, for the sake of strengthening the learning ability in each level.

On models of learning, one must understand that learning is not only cognitive, but emotional and behavioral. People need to understand the new learning and feel it is right to adopt these new assumptions into their routines, where knowing, feeling and acting have to be balanced. A learning culture is investment in technology, infrastructure, development of people, but it is also related to trust that members of the group/organization have in each other and in the management, and where they will not feel insecure or become victims of their own learning.

The types of learning, the central issue is the type of problem solving process that makes sense in a given difficulty situation. A simple error correction can generate an outcome, but the reflex action that questions the assumptions and the personal and group point of view causes learning to suggest more significant changes in the organization functioning, able to change the fundamental rules of a particular work process.

Finally, the learning process is understood as the backbone of Organizational Learning from four not necessarily sequential steps: (i) information identification which seems to be important for learning and creation (generation) of a new knowledge; (ii) the exchange, dissemination or distribution of knowledge in the individual and collective levels; (iii) the integration of knowledge between system levels (individual, collective, organizational) in which the changes can be adopted in each of them or several at the same time and finally (iv) the transformation in new knowledge that can be applied in the organizational routines producing effects on organizational behavior (development of a new style of leadership, a new product) (Figure 3).

Figure 3 - Simplified Model of Organizational Learning Process.

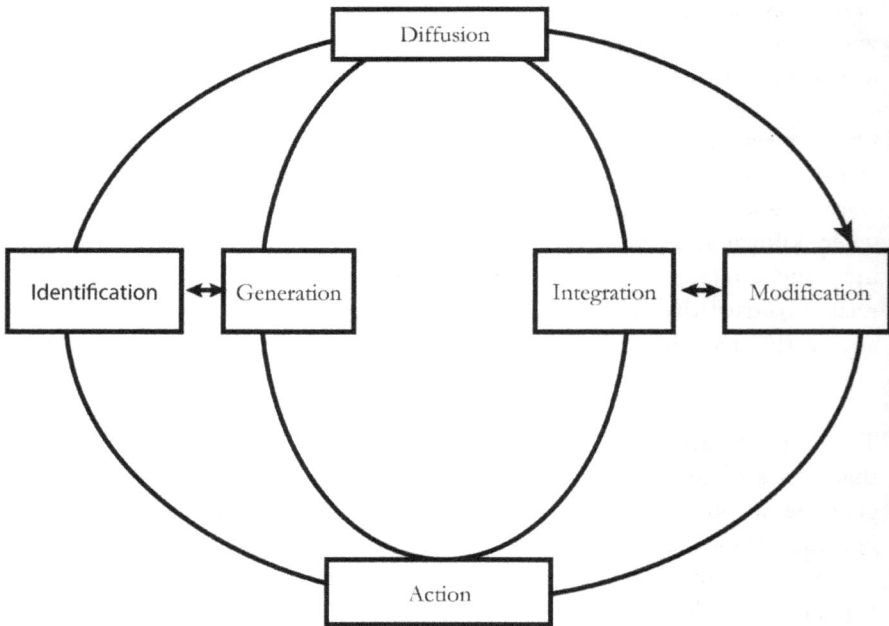

Source: Pawlowsky (2001, p. 79)

However, there are the following questions: Who is responsible for collecting information on the environment? Which information is able to generate new learning ? Which individuals or groups have access to the knowledge generated? What experiences and knowledge are the core of the business? How are the experiences arranged and combined to generate new knowledge? How should they store the new learning: in the people's memory, in learning histories, in databases, in any other way or combination? What model of communication is used to disseminate new learning?

They are reflections that find responses, even in construction, on the theory presented below. Proposition that underlies the forms and the structuring of knowledge management in contemporary organizations, and also the principles of corporate education, with systematic education at all levels of organizational structure.

According to Hirotaka Takeuchi and Ikujiro Nonaka, the organizational learning processes, as a creator of new knowledge, happen from the inside out in organizations oriented to learning, enabling to redefine problems and solutions. Thus, as stated by Peter Pawlowsky, organizations with guidance for learning are less susceptible to environmental forces, because they change the business environment in which they operate. They actually create new knowledge and information, from the inside out, aiming to redefine both problems as the solutions and in the process, recreate its environment.

Figure 4 - Bases of knowledge creation process.

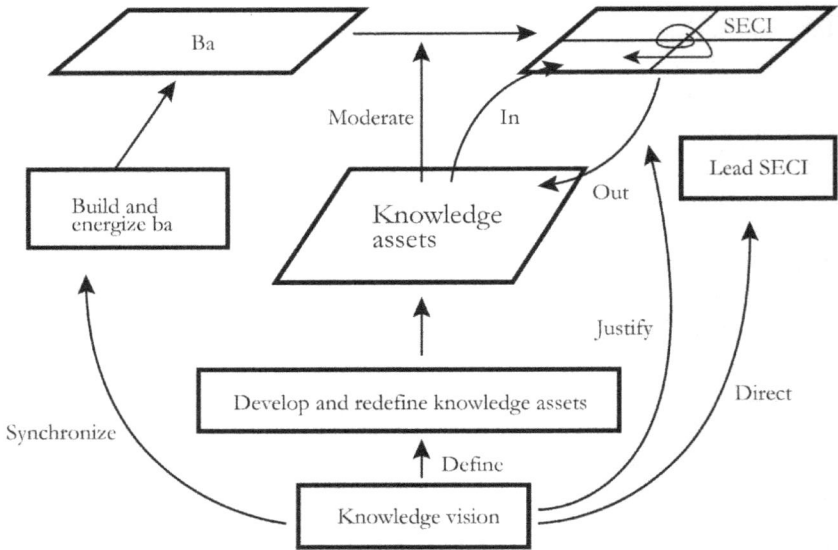

Source: Nonaka, Toyama and Byosière (2005, p 493).

Knowledge, therefore, is related to a specific context situations, dependent of situations and propitious moments. It is dynamic and therefore created in the social dynamics. It is human and it has in its nature the action and subjectivity incorporated in the commitments and beliefs that are rooted in the individual value system.

To understand how organizations create knowledge and develop learning, Hirotaka Takeuchi and Ikujiro Nonaka, Noburo Knno and Ryoko Tayoma developed the model of organizational knowledge creation situated on three bases of interaction and complementarity. The bases are: platforms for knowledge creation - *Ba* - the conversion modes of knowledge - SECI (socialization, externalization, combination and internalization) -, and the inputs and outputs of knowledge as essential resources to the creation of value to organizations - *Knowledge Assets.*

The SECI model is developed based on the theory of creation of organizational knowledge, in the relationship between the epistemological and ontological dimensions of knowledge. This theory is based on four knowledge conversion modes from the interaction between tacit and explicit knowledge. Organizational knowledge is created in the interaction between tacit and explicit knowledge, alternating in four combinations. This understanding is based on the distinction between these two types of knowledge, but complementary to each other and with exchange in all the activities of creation and expansion of knowledge, carried out by humans in their productive activities.

The process of organizational learning and knowledge creation in organizations are located in the dynamic interactions between tacit and explicit knowledge. This interaction occurs through the spiral of knowledge and, as the catchment areas located in each quadrant of the model are being used, it widens the level of knowledge - of the individual to the interorganization.

Socialization is a form of externalization of tacit knowledge through the exchange of experiences into the context of emotions and situations. Externalization involves the conceptualization, elaboration of the hypotheses, analogies or models presentation, but mainly by the ability to reflect that this knowledge field provides. The combination passing through the formal process of knowledge which, in its reconfiguring capacity, can lead to new knowledge. Internalization is the result of the process of incorporation of other modes of knowledge conversion, resulting in the broader sphere of the spiral, reaching organizational and inter-organizational dimension.

Figure 5 - Knowledge conversion modes.

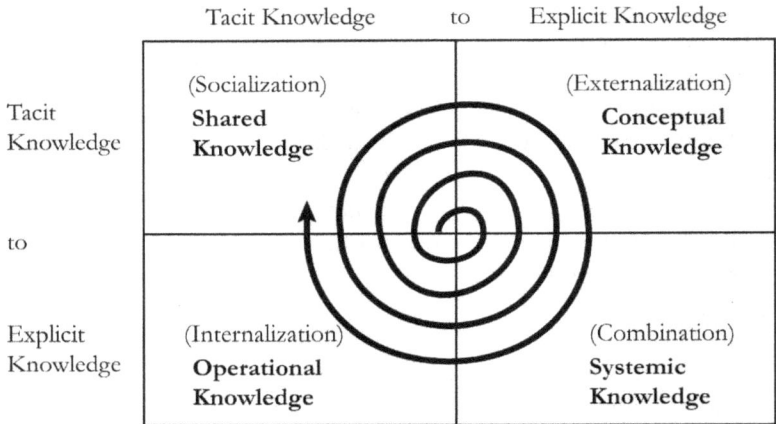

	Tacit Knowledge	to	Explicit Knowledge
Tacit Knowledge	(Socialization) **Shared Knowledge**		(Externalization) **Conceptual Knowledge**
to			
Explicit Knowledge	(Internalization) **Operational Knowledge**		(Combination) **Systemic Knowledge**

Source: Adapted from Nonaka and Takeuchi (2008, p. 60)

Socialization is a form of externalization of tacit knowledge through the exchange of experiences into the context of emotions and specific situations. Externalization involves the conceptualization, elaborates hypotheses, analogies or models presentation, but mainly by the ability to reflect that this knowledge field provides. The combination passing through the formal process of knowledge which, in its reconfiguring capacity, can lead to new knowledge. Internalization is the result of the process of incorporation of other modes of knowledge conversion, resulting in the broader sphere of the spiral, reaching organizational and inter-organizational dimension.

Thus, the organizational knowledge creation process is divided into five phases.

Figure 6 - Model of five phases of the creation of organizational knowledge process.

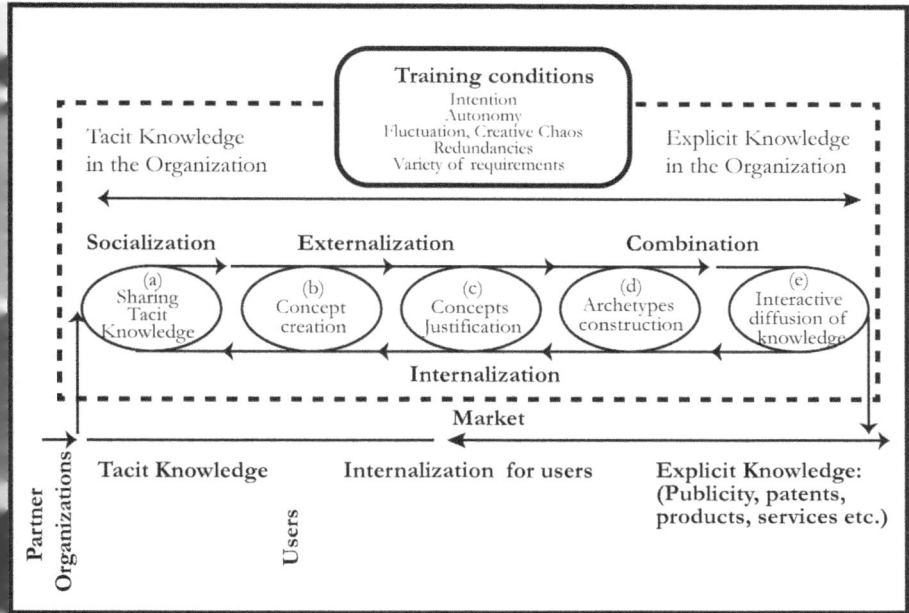

Source: Takeuchi and Nonaka (2008, p 82).

Thus, the process of organizational knowledge creation begins with the sharing of tacit knowledge, which roughly corresponds to socialization because the rich and untapped knowledge that resides in individuals must be first amplified in the organization. The establishment process of organizational knowledge begins in order to be shared by the group of individuals, becoming something that should be known to all, regardless of its content.

In the second phase, the shared tacit knowledge, for example, by a self-organized staff is converted to explicit knowledge in the form of a new concept, a similar process to externalization. At this stage, the knowledge, previously shared, assumes an aggregator role and becomes a "new concept", assimilated in principle by all. Thus, the concept created must be justified in the third stage, in which the organization determines whether the new concept is worth seeking.

Thus, this new concept needs to be validated, in its understanding by the group, from the same "is worth seeking." Receiving the continuity message, the concepts are converted in the fourth stage in an archetype, which may take the form of a prototype for the case a "concrete" product development; or in an operating mechanism, such as "abstract" innovations as a new corporate value, a new administrative system or an innovative organizational structure.

Here, according to the authors, this concept is already adapted to the organizational culture of the group, and therefore a "new corporate value," being by all accepted. The last phase extends the knowledge created, for example, in a department to the others in the department, through other departments, or even by external constituents in what we call leveling of knowledge. These external components include customers, affiliates, universities and distributors. A company creator of knowledge does not operate in a closed system, but in an open system in which knowledge is constantly exchanged with the external environment.

These five conditions promote the process of knowledge creation, and facilitate the learning flow, ownership and use of knowledge by individuals, groups/teams and organization, reflecting the state of being of the knowledge organization, value creation and advantages for means innovations, either in processes or in products.

The basis of this process, the SECI, is the *ba*. *Ba* can be translated roughly as the place where knowledge is shared, created and used, understanding that organizational knowledge needs an order to exist. The concept of *ba* is not limited to physical space, but is in the context of virtual, mental space, or in combination of these spaces. Its main feature is sustained on the concept of interaction.

The *Ba* area origination refers to the space in which individuals share their emotions, feelings, experiences and mental models. It serves to strengthen relations and establish a behavior of synchronization through exchange of experiences. The *Ba* dialog area, based on peer contact, it is presented reflective due to interaction with a focus on specific knowledge.

Figure 7 - Sharing knowledge space - Socialization /Externalization.

	Socilization	Externalization	
Face to face	Originating *Ba* (Existential)	Dialoguing *Ba* (Reflective)	**Peer-to-peer**
Site	Exercising *Ba* (Synthetic)	Systematizing *Ba* (Systemic)	**Collaboration (Group)**
	Internalization	Combination	

Source: Adapted Nonaka, Toyama and Byosière (2001, p 498.).

Mental models and individual competencies are converted into common terms and concepts, where people share from the mental model of the other, but they have the ability to analyze and reflect their own models. The *ba* systematization can be understood as the combination phase of new explicit knowledge, systematizing them in the practice of the organization. The *ba* exercising phase is based on the internalization and facilitates the transformation of explicit knowledge into tacit knowledge. The exercise of continuity promotes continuous learning through self improvement centered on labor standards.

Finally, the *Knowledge Assets* are the inputs and outputs in the creation of knowledge as a factor of moderation, influencing the functions of *Ba*. This is the intellectual capital as specific resource of the companies that are indispensable for creating value.

Knowledge assets are also categorized into quadrants, whose representation is given based on experiential, conceptual, systemic and routinized knowledge. The experiential knowledge is supported on sharing experiences among members of the organization (teams, subsidiaries, suppliers and customers), setting it on specific assets of the company, which makes imitation possibilities difficult .The assets of conceptual knowledge are articulated in the set of images, signs, symbols, brand, products and others, built through the externalization process.

Figure 8 - Knowledge sharing space.

Assets of Experiential Knowledge	Assets of Conceptual Knowledge
Tacit knowledge shared through common experiences.	Explicit knowledge articulated by images, symbols and language.
-Individual Skill and *"know-how"*;	-Concepts of products;
-Care, love, trust and security;	-*Design*;
-Energy, passion and tension.	-Brand value.
Assets of Habitual Knowledge (routinized)	**Assets of Systemic Knowledge**

Tacit knowledge routinized and incorporated through common experiences. - "*Know-how*" in daily operations; -Organizational routine; -Organizational culture.	Systematization and framework of explicit knowledge. -Documents, specifications, manuals, etc; -Data, information, software; -Licenses and patents.

Source: Adapted Nonaka, Toyama and Byosière (2001, p 502.).

The systemic knowledge is represented by technology, patents, licenses, product specifications, manuals and informational documents on customers and suppliers. It refers to the stage of facilitated dissemination and transfer of the assets; however, it is less significant as a competitive advantage, unless it becomes legal protection. Knowledge assets routinized in the organization are represented by actions and practices developed in the management , production, communication, among others activities. It is how to make the execution, processes, businesses. The routines are created and shared by the organization in the internalization process.

Through continuous exercise, certain patterns of thinking and actions are enhanced and shared within the organization. Therefore, the assets of routinized knowledge is practical knowledge. Sharing [plots] of events and 'stories' of the company also help form the routinized knowledge. Thus, the three bases of organizational knowledge creation, SECI, *Ba* and *Knowledge Assets*, converge to the association of knowledge and learning at all levels of the organization, enabling the sense of value perceived by *stakeholders*.

CHAPTER 5
CORPORATE EDUCATION AND SERVICES: CONVERGENCES

The service sector differs from those ones of production of goods, having quite peculiar characteristics, in which each requires well-defined strategies to achieving the targets. The main features are: the intangibility - the service can not be seen, tasted, felt, heard or smelled before buying; indivisibility [inseparability] - can not be separated from its suppliers; variability - the quality of service depends on who provides them, when, where and how they are provided; and perishability - can not be stored for sale and further use.

Therefore some different characteristics bring different problems faced by other productive sectors. In that respect, the human element is crucial to the efficiency of operations, due to the inevitable interaction between provider and client, source of great opportunities, but difficult to be controlled. Thus, nothing could be more appropriate than investing in competencies, human development and education of workers, as organizational advantage, because during the whole process of production and sale of the service, they will be the most conspicuous mark of the company.

On these terms, the worker competencies become more important because given the conditions in which occur service activities, nothing is more prominent than the customer perception regarding quality measurement criteria, the main subject of the effectiveness of activity work. Thus, according to the flow of production efficiency *versus* the opportunities in providing services (FIG. 1), even in more technocratic ways, the competencies and expertise of workers in this segment are the ones that make a difference in production and service provision, because it is a productive activity performed by people for other people, whose humanistic perception can not be ruled out.

This means that the greater the interaction with the customer, such as the service industry, the greater the demands for qualifications are. This might result in differentials in the processor to satisfy the needs. Therefore, the higher the personalized service, the greater the demands for expertise and capabilities to respond the emerging demands of direct contact.

Figure 1 - Productive efficiency *versus* opportunities in service delivery.

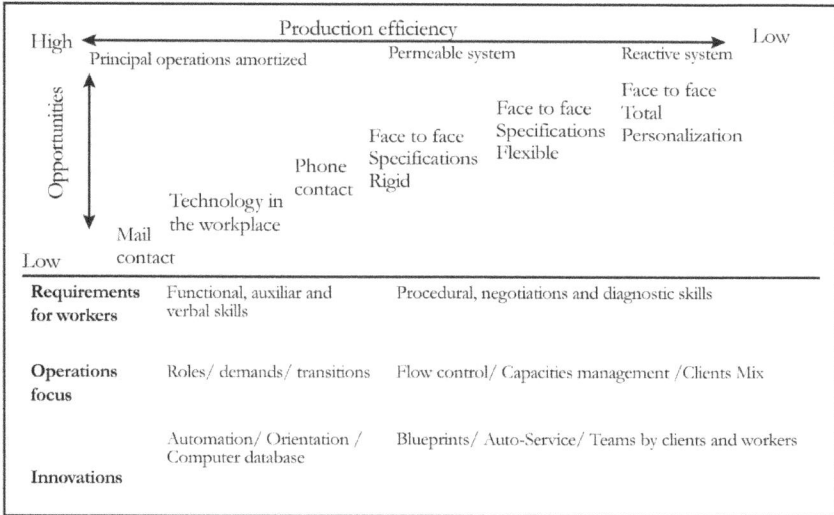

High ←	Production efficiency				→ Low
	Principal operations amortized	Permeable system		Reactive system	
Opportunities ↕				Face to face Total Personalization	Face to face Total Personalization
				Face to face Specifications Flexible	
		Phone contact	Face to face Specifications Rigid		
	Technology in the workplace				
Low	Mail contact				

Requirements for workers	Functional, auxiliar and verbal skills	Procedural, negotiations and diagnostic skills
Operations focus	Roles/ demands/ transitions	Flow control/ Capacities management /Clients Mix
Innovations	Automation/ Orientation / Computer database	Blueprints/ Auto-Service/ Teams by clients and workers

Source: Adapted from Fitzsimmons and Fitzsimmons (2000, p. 108).

The higher the personalized service, the lower the production efficiency will be. The more contact, the greater the opportunities will be, then the corporate education should play its role to develop critical competencies both in the expansion opportunities, as in the productive performance, to leverage organizational efficiency to those service providers.

To resume, the basic competencies of the business environment based on changes over the responsibility in the learning process, working together so that each employee becomes more competent in their activity and inherent matter. Therefore, they would have the lead on the activity and guidance in the integration of complementary activities. All this would then reflect in economic benefits to the organization. It is understood that is transforming the worker into the job manager, giving him more autonomy and increasing his commitment to work and career, and consequently with the team and the organization's results.

This approach perfectly accepts the outlook for understanding the organizational learning and the use of platforms for action ventures in the corporate education systems. It is not enough, by organizations, to have focused on the characteristics, the needs or the learning properties, but also in the compound of people who interrelate. However, it is necessary to integrate the information provided by each approach, aiming to achieve the development continuation more in line with the dynamic of education requirements, personalized for each family of positions or functions, able to create a favorable improvement and innovation environment for processes and services, as also in the management modes.

Therefore the basic organizational competencies are: (i) learning to learn -the agent's openness to learning throughout the process, understanding that within service, there is no opportunity for subsequent correction; (ii) communication and collaboration -the quality of the dialogue with the receptor is critical to satisfactory results; (iii) the creative and decisive reasoning -during the provision of service there is no time for long breaks after the start; (iv) technological knowledge -an inherent part of the process and can contribute to the satisfaction and excellence in the service provided; (v) business knowledge -the expertise on what is done; (vi) leadership development and (vii) self-management career, strongly desirable in such services dynamic sector.

The learning process, which is embodied in the application capability of individuals, may be understood in seven interdependent and further subdivisions that are significant when the involvement of the service provider agent in the relationship with the client is as great as the need to develop such competencies. It would allow then the neutralization any possibility of failure, and the expansion of success opportunities.

Resuming the mentioned competency, the ability to learn to learn: the link is in asking the right questions, identifying the essence of complex ideas, finding ways to measure the knowledge and applying specific techniques to the goals of each task at the office, identifying what is needed to know and the ability to do it. Also, the attitudes needed to take so it is learned what is needed, and the obstacles, resources and perspectives are identified. To finish with this process, the learning performance is assessed.

Learn to learn is the base for all other competencies. Since it is in the integration of disciplines inherent in mental models, the formation of a common goal to the development of group learning, systems thinking and personal domain. All this based on the essence, principle and practice, even with subtle but important differences, which all converge towards the common factor, sensitivity of learners in an intrinsically interdependent world. Interdependence is the core process of service delivery, which incorporates the usefulness perceived by the customer as a result of participation of everyone involved in the process.

With this, there are personal and organizational factors that either facilitate or hinder the learning administration in organizations, in teams and individuals. Among the factors that facilitate, there is encouragement to identify personal learning needs and setting goals, review and feedback of performance and learning, learning perception in assisting in the workplace and promoting experiences that stimulate the development, tolerance of mistakes, and encouragement of review and planning, challenge the traditional way of doing things, which is a common practice in innovative enterprises.

On the other hand, the ones that discourage the learning transit on two poles, personal and organizational as to the former are related to perceptions of the learning need and competencies, beliefs, values, emotions, mental intellectual ability, age, memory and communication competencies. The second concerns the form of internal organization of work, organizational development systems, culture and climate, decision-making, policy and risk aversion, instability and change, economic status, competition, power and control.

As for communication and collaboration, there is evidence that supports the quality of interdependent relationships, demonstrating -in flow situation- the emerging knowledge capabilities of workers´ communities. However, they are competencies generally not learned at schools, and this deficiency requires organizations to provide this educational absence, causing the common sense of purpose and need to know in each member group. Corporate education should stimulate creative and problem-solving capacity established in learning groups and, based on actions and simulations, evaluate business strategies and suggest solutions in real time. Undeniably, the use of technological resources is a more practical and agile way for organizations to disseminate information and knowledge.

The last two basic competencies cited by Jeanne Meister, leadership development and career self-management, refer to the dimension of development encouraged by the organization that supports the gap filling in previous education. Leadership development and career self-management enable a 'flight plan' mapped in the strategic planning of required competencies, to encourage the employee in looking after his career due to changes in the environment possibilities and organizational structure, to further adapt to changes.

CHAPTER 6
INNOVATION: INTEGRATION SHAFT

Setting up a theoretical concept for innovation has a number of definitions with some similarities, but many of them have objected about the completeness of the conceptual construct. There are specific and inherent aspects in the interpretation of the concept, whose scope is limited to the fragment approach: technological and organizational innovation, production, management and others.

In a way, this can compromise the concept operating process, but it contrastingly gives opening for the meaning abstraction about its characteristics, forms, principles and practices. It gives scope to the meanings when innovation is presented as the core process of the organization, and not represented by departments; everyone's responsibility is required contribution for the organization's performance. It is not about technology or production, but value, opportunity and impact on the market. Innovation is not invention, and the terminology to be used is not technology but economy. This is to safeguard the association commonly found in textbooks about innovation. Therefore, the concept is completed by Joseph Schumpeter when he defines innovation as: "[...] simply do new things or do the same things in a different way."

Innovation can have its focus on action. Innovation is the use of new technological knowledge and/or market, whose aim is a new service or product to be offered to consumers. It is contextualized in the set of organizational competencies supported on the creative capacity of its various value chain activities, converging thus to run the concept, defining it around the production and dividing it into four forms represented, also by action as: a new product, a new method or mode of production, a new market or a new production organization.

A breakthrough is understood in the concept of innovation as action, adding the idea that to achieve innovation, there is action to be taken to introduce something new, and it can be understood from the perspective of the user. In this way, innovation refers to the post-creation process until the effective use by users. For the author, the definition can lead to a variety of ways - a product, a behavior, a system, a process, a business model - but at their heart all have the idea that when put into practice, introduction might occur and initiate the process of innovation.

This idea supports the view that innovation has a comprehensive process and understands steps from conception to the consumer of the product or service, beyond the invention or innovation, focusing on different sectors and in many times, reinforcing its concept available to the consumption and in a large scale.

Concerning to its conceptual understanding, innovation is a creative action, that is embedded in what is new or as improvement on what is existing. It can be incremental or radical, and it has to represent to consumers or users the introduction of something new and available. It may be product, service , technological process, system or administrative structure, project or relationship program.

It's worth pointing out that there is still a specific limit on the concept by economic theorists and those of organizational studies. Economists usually define innovation as a new process or practice in the industry, emphasizing a speed of innovation in relation to each other; but the organizational theorists, in another thought, usually focus on the products or processes that are new to the company, emphasizing the magnitude of innovation. However, even with these differences in perception of each of the areas, the commitment of the concept is not shown, focusing only on the different ways of viewing the same object, but in a complementary manner.

There are two other important aspects to be emphasized in the definition of innovation. First, the recurrent association of the term innovation to learning and knowledge which is translated into the qualitative combination of know-how in human assets and organizational competencies accumulated throughout its existence. Thus, the conceptual association of innovation with learning is related to two aspects, both in the inherent actions related to the creation or increase, and in the introduction matters - capacity utilization by the subjects.

Therefore, as stated by Faiz Gallouj, the myths and the specificities of innovation in the service sector should be considered. Related to this, the author discusses that "[...] the inertia of analytical equipments inherited from agricultural and industrial economies [...]", when it's refuted, it becomes capable "[...] to reconcile the two major features of the modern economy [...] ": service and innovation.

Due to the fact that the realities are different from each other, the innovation is considerable in the services sector, being related to an inverse process to the industrial sector in relation to the customer. This relationship clearly shows some reversal of power relations or inter-sector domination.

It is the attempt to find or develop a comprehensive analysis of the technological and non-technological approach in innovation, however without sacrificing the importance of one over the other. However, the concept of innovation with inherent claims in the service sector is still insufficient in revealing the riches that innovation manifested in services, either on the methodological aspects, or in the results.

The universe of companies has determinant singularities, however, in all fields of business activity, there are the logical of economic, political and market (dis) regulations, among many others. Within this scope, changes are noticeable to each of them in the environment in which companies operate. Their ability to deal with the instability underpins their existence and continuity. From this point of view, the enterprising has two functions: *marketing* and innovation. Therefore, the interest on innovation, for the business scope, appears as a motivator for the effectiveness of this function, to unveil its forms, aspects and features in line with market dynamics and economic expansion.

This is a suggestive reflection of incorporating changes, considered naturally and desirable to consumer needs. Thus, the applicability of economic principles to the organization is subject to environmental factors that determine the categories of business, circumscribed in uncertainty and unpredictability.

As pointed by Cristina Lemos, that approach emphasizes the "[...] neo-Schumpeterian approach that points to a close relationship between economic growth and changes that occur with the introduction and dissemination of technological and organizational innovations. It is understood, from this point of view, that advances resulting from innovative processes are a basic factor in the formation of transformation patterns of economy as well as its long-term development. "

In the context of the global economy, companies have to be committed to innovation as the same intensity as they agree with the market positioning, because the former is a prerequisite for the second. When companies are geared only to the market, dissociated to innovation, they may suffer major risks, especially when it reaches the prominent status, since in general, that feeling often cherish until the numbness. In contrast, if the orientation were to the commitment with the innovation (measuring the impact and the importance to the company's business) the likelihood of numbness, if it's not zero, it retreats.

Seeking to increase the understanding of the characteristics of business innovation over the past decades, Roy Rothwell presents that the business model innovation is divided in five generations. The first refers to the period between the 1950s and 1960s, when the demand was higher than production and claimed by technological innovations and production management; this was called innovation pushed by technology. In the 1960s and 1970s, with the increased competitiveness and before developing technological solutions to meet the needs of consumers, companies began to make sure about the demands before producing - the period of innovation driven by the market.

The compound of innovation model comprises the 1970s and 1980s, when the business innovation process was characterized by a complex communication path linking the internal and external actors, to gain access to knowledge in the scientific community and the market. In the 1980s and 1990s with Japanese people initiatives, the integration between various functional company departments was launched, in order to generate innovations more quickly through activities conducted in parallel; this was the so-called integrated model.

Thus, innovation is a process of networks that can be seen in its external appearance in strategic alliances, cooperation and integration business, but also from the multi-functionality of the internal teams in a process of acquiring and sharing knowledge along a production line.

This understanding is shared especially with regards to the organizational dimension manifested in the creation of innovation networks, which characterizes the combined action of various actors in the complex and non-linear articulation of specific competencies necessary for the innovation outbreak.

There are essentially three types of innovation for all companies: in product or service, in the localization market and behavior and values of customers, and in various competencies and activities necessary to produce the goods and services to bring them to market. They can be respectively called product innovation, social innovation (for example: sale to the provision), and administrative innovation.

Naturally, the commitment to innovation within companies must be permeated throughout the organization. Through production and selection of knowledge, it would meet the demands for new or improved products, services, technological processes, systems or administrative structure, projects or relationship programs. However, this is not distant from organizational strategies, giving foundation to interactivity among the culture of innovation, the alignment of priorities, the use of available resources and trade capacity, and going back to the original purpose which is the service customer needs.

It is understood then that business innovation is sustained by a triad of values, which aligned to market needs, can be revealed in networks, the corporate commitment to the culture of innovation and knowledge as a decisive action for the occurrence business innovation, either gradual or radical.

A 'knowledge-based' vision focuses on the interactive processes through which knowledge is created and exchanged within and between firms and other organizations. Many knowledge-intensive industries such as high technology manufacturing and business services have strongly grown in many developed economies. [...] Although the R&D vitally works in the innovation process, many innovative activities are not based on R&D, even though they depend on highly skilled workers, interactions with other firms and public research institutions, and an organizational structure that leads to learning and exploitation of knowledge.

It can be said that companies that wish to have good innovative performance need the commitment to a culture of improvement, with the constant maintenance of knowledge through learning. Consequently, the development of organizational and human competencies constitutes actions alliances, partnerships and sharing in order to proactively support themselves in the market. This understanding emphasizes the creation of organizational knowledge as a key point for continuous innovation processes, where there is, in the case of innovative companies, beliefs and specific organizational commitment to innovation. This knowledge is generated with some purpose related to the action and to the context of its relational existence, which strengthens the foundations of generated knowledge, resulting in gradual or radical innovation.

The analysis about innovative companies and the features that shape them does not appear to be simplistic or homogeneous, but they set different behaviors and actions applied to one end: the development and implementation of new ideas, aiming to achieve the desired results, with people who are engaged in transactions with others to change their institutional and organizational contexts.

It is possible to assume from the previous reference that people are responsible for this process, which was the main innovation driver. The base is knowledge, and the value is created by productivity and innovation, which are knowledge applications to work. This guidance states that innovative firms tend to invest in generation, appropriation and dissemination of knowledge in all spheres of its structure. This understanding assumes the innovation processes are encapsulated through the learning process, being influenced by the organizational structure, the communicative practices and the social context. As an idea moves from its inception and throughout its development and implementation, it is people within the organization who push, modify or suspend innovation. Their behavior, which is the result of a process of adaptive and interactive learning, is affected by contextual factors.

The OSLO Manual shows that innovative companies tend to take innovation as a system that has the transfer and dissemination of ideas, experiences and knowledge as a center that is inserted in social, political and cultural organizations. Innovation is seen as a dynamic process in which knowledge is accumulated through learning and interaction.

Therefore, it is possible to outline organizations through their structure, communication practices, the information circulation and the segment in which they operate. They find facilitating factors or inhibitors of innovation, but the learning and the proper management of knowledge are determining factors for classifying whether a company is innovative or not.

Thus, in the current context of intense competition it is recognized that knowledge is the fundamental basis and interactive learning, the best way for individuals, companies, regions and countries to be able to cope with the changes in progress, intensify the generation of innovations and prepare into a more positive insertion at this stage.

The innovative capacity of the company depends on the whole, not simply on the organizational formats that favor innovation through R&D´s departments; being in isolation does not guarantee good performance, and therefore it would reinforce the idea that the generation of business innovation capacity is linked to the management capacity information and knowledge throughout the enterprise system. Thus, companies focused on innovation adjust their efforts to the development of people, while less innovative ones direct their resources for the immobilization of capital goods in external acquisitions. So companies focused on innovation demonstrate that the concern for training professionals can leverage innovation.

It is understood then that innovative companies tend to establish close relationship with the management of organizational knowledge, strongly inserted in the two dimensions of competencies: individual and organizational. Both of them differ in the remaining scope, and they are still closely related to learning processes that similarly exist on the individual and organizational levels.

Therefore, when speaking of innovative features, the dimensions of knowledge, learning and education as a means to promote core competencies are embedded in the entire scope of the organization and, as previously discussed, they are assumed to be strategies to achieve goals.

5.1 Innovation in Services

For a long time, services were not considered an innovative activity, they just adopted innovations occurring in other sectors. However, with the evidence that the services sector has gained in recent decades, studies have shown that its innovation framework appears less cloudy than expected.

Researches such as Anthony Arundel and Hugo Hollanders show that innovation in the service sector, excluding the public sector, demonstrates superiority over other sectors, for example, transport and storage, supply of electricity, gas and water, wholesale and trade (except the automobile industry), among others. Of all the various studies, there is an emerging consensus that services innovate, both in terms of products as processes, and even some services, are at the forefront of innovation. But what this represents?

Here comes the issues raised when revealing the problems involved with the research methods in innovation in the service sector. The two methodological guidelines presented by the first author and often adopted in this type of research have shortcomings regarding the effectiveness on containing the nuances related to the wealth of actions that the sector offers. The second author suggests that it is needed to refine the concepts, the data capture instruments and methodologies for measuring innovation for the consolidation of the results presented.

However, even within this deficit methodological context, both innovation in the service sector, as the growth of participation in the world economy are becoming more popular in research and studies about organizational innovation. This represents the importance of conducting research to develop appropriate methodologies to this sector which has quite different characteristics from the others. In this industry, innovation can encompass four types: innovation on the product (service), process, *marketing*, and management or organizational.This is due to the fact that services both innovates radically as incrementally, with an innovation most often perceived on management models.

These results support the view of innovation in services as an interactive and incremental process, that depends on the relationship between companies and other agents such as professional services providers and clients. This view is consistent with concepts such as organizational learning, innovation on networks, tacit knowledge and interactive learning, discussed by authors whose subject of study is not specifically the service sector.

In this reflective orientation, it is fitted questions about the reasons for the low perception of innovation in services: the first is that technology, by itself, does not play key role in service companies; the competencies and competencies of staff result in a central role in providing service. Second, with complex administrative systems, the operations are not planned enough and, when deploying technological systems in already existent operations, the companies tend to do it in processes and activities that would be better performed manually.

These problem-issues of innovation in services address aspects such as the involvement of multiple actors in the process of service delivery and the heterogeneity on the implementation of services, that are reflected substantially in the way how the processes, products (services) and management models are operationalized on the day-to-day of organizations.

The development of services in the enterprise level is not necessarily a result of deliberate development initiatives, budgets in the field of technology and definetly not necessarily driven by economic reasons. In many cases, it is a consequence, for example, of the heterogeneity of requests from clients or a consequence of institutional change. Innovation on services is considered as a subset of service development. So, when exploring the development of services in order to understand the service innovation, it should be understood from the outside or dual approach [from the inside out and the outside in] regarding to innovation .

It expresses the relationship between client-producer of the service, even considering the specificities of each sector of services and the degree of intensity of contact and knowledge, it enables innovation opportunities of the service provided. It includes production and process, resulting in superior technological innovations processes and products. This reveals the proposal to create value in the relationship of service delivery. While innovation can be understood from the introduction of the service in the market, making the service available to the client, its intensity is seen under the aspects of customer value creation and long-term results for the organization. Innovations in services would be, from that perspective, the result of interaction processes in which success would depend on the level of knowledge of actors and their relationship competencies.

Thus, the propositions on service innovation are complex, but it is possible to capture the development of its action in the practice of organizations. Therefore, in a proposal of advances in studies and research in this sector, it is clear that evolution is conditioned to the do, since in each new element raised, it is possible to bring contributions to the development of methodologies and approaches that add value and make them more effective.

Thus, this theoretical set ends with a synthesis that has the purpose to demonstrate the features that bring the approaches used to contextualize this case studied (Table 4).

Table 4 - Summary Theoretical.

Features	Corporate Education	Learning and Organizational Knowledge	Innovation
Competencies	It is based in management competencies and aims to improve organizational effectiveness, contributing to the achievement of the company's strategies.	It is located in intermediation between learning and individual and the collective knowledge, ordering them for specific purposes to the performance of activities inherent in the function or position and in increasing or improving outcomes through interactions between levels organizational system.	Way of acting opposite to what is done or what can be done, so that result in innovations in management, product (goods / service), in the process and /or marketing, radical or incremental manner.
Competencies	Acts on the individual or family roles, formally or informally, whenever there is a demand for competencies development, at any time or physical space.	Acts at all levels of the system, including processes, types and models of learning, organizing the knowledge so that it becomes accessible within the interests of the organization.	Act on the development, deployment or implementation of new ideas that enable more effective results in the production or market share.
Results	It operates in the personal development of employees, generating an increase in work performance.	Enables the creation and sharing of knowledge to justify its application and validation in the work process.	Results in a new product, a new method of management, a new mode of production, a new market of operation and / or a new organization of production.

Source: Research data, in 2011.

CHAPTER 7
THE STUDIED CASE

This chapter makes a brief presentation of the studied company, highlighting the relevant characteristics for this research. The presentation is divided in general characteristics, BPTC Brazil, Regional Office in Minas Gerais, RO-MG, and specific corporate education in the searched regional board.

The post office in Brazil was founded in 1663, based on a system of totally disorganized postal activities and no formal guarantees of execution services. However, after three centuries, in 1969 by Law No. 509, the Brazilian Post and Telegraph Company (BPTC) was launched, being a public company linked to the Ministry of Communications, having a service model that remains until today even with the changes.

The organizational structure of the Post Office comprises the ordered set of responsibilities, authorities, hierarchical obligations, functions and descriptive areas and organs. It is represented by the central government, comprising the Supervisory Board, the Board of Directors, the Board, the Executive Committee, Departments, service centers and agencies of the same level, and the Regional Directors, composed by the Regional Directors.

Its service operates in two parts: the monopolized sector (Decree-Law No. 509/69, ratified by Law No. 6,538 / 78), including letter, postcard, grouped mail and telegram; and non monopolized services, as orders, transport and distribution of products, receipt of payment of bills and taxes, enrollment in contests and other services. These services focus on two customer profiles, individuals and legal entities. Among them, postal and philatelic services and products and convenience services are highlighted.

On its numbers, as disclosed in its annual report 2009, the company had 108,220 employees distributed in administrative (14%) and operational (86%). activities. BPTC had 6,257 branches of service, 32 philatelic agencies, 238 licensees agencies, 1,401 franchised agencies, 3,344 community agencies, 6466 product sales points and 22,561 collection boxes.

Thus, the company appears with high degree of public confidence in researches about the brand value, demonstrating that the scandal involving employees in 2006 did not shake the popular opinion as shown in the 2008 survey, in which the brand value is above the national currency and the Brazilian Armed Forces as brands.

The Regional Office of Minas Gerais (ROMG) of the Brazilian Post and Telegraph Company (BPTC) serves 853 municipalities, with 10,630 employees and 2,642 contractors. It has as operations structure 3,693 branches, 154 distribution centers and one central integrated logistics.

Management strategies are focused on three pillars. **Business** is focused on appropriate solutions to customers converging in profitability for the company. In 2009, the company entered into a thousand new contracts with corporate customers and achieved operating income of 7.5% over the previous. The organizational part is based on a proposal of integration, motivation and employee satisfaction for the achievement of organizational goals. It is supported by recognition policies, employee participation in innovation processes, improving the working environment and investment in health, as well as investments in training and development through its Corporate Education center. Finally, there are the **social responsibility** actions that are developed actions such as selective collection, collection of cells and batteries, use of environmentally friendly fuel for the entire fleet used by the company, sponsorship of sports and cultural activities, among others.

Seeking the expertise of its people and the improvement of quality in the services provided to its customers, the BPTC was concerned with the education of its workers. After a year of establishment, the Post and Telegraph Company established two formation agencies for staff training and development. At that time, there was a division in teaching staff performing functions that required higher education, the School of Postal Administration (ESAP) and education for entry-level, middle and technical, the Human Resources Department (HRD), with all regions representation.

In two decades, this educational model has proved insufficient, leaving gaps in the alignment of educational programs to the company's strategies. The

BPTC increased operating revenues intended for educational activities and matured the idea of deploying a single orientation of business education sector. These factors, coupled with the proliferation of corporate universities in the national and international scene, made possible to create the Corporate University of Posts (UNICO) in December 2001. The main objective had the task of unifying the educational activities within the company and project them to the entire value chain.

Today, a decade later, UNICO keeps its initial assumptions, based on the concept of enterprise learning; it is establishing itself as a reference in terms of training and development of postal service professionals. It encompasses all educational activities and impacts the entire organizational structure, contractors, customers, suppliers, regulators and postal operators, partners, international organizations and the community, in order to advertise its culture and values.

The principles that guide its actions are integrated into a participatory and collaborative environment that seeks to share relevant information to the achievement of the company objectives, and defines the attitudes of the corporate university , and how it suggests to carry out the organization's concerns based on permanent education. The principles are:

1) The fundamental ethical principles of University Post are equality, citizenship, integrity, professionalism, balance, tolerance and commitment to results.

2) It is the duty of the University to value cultural diversity, defend pluralism of ideas, encourage research and creativity in order to create conditions of its target audience continuous education.

3) The University performance should be transparent and maintain commitment to truth.

4) It is up to all who attend the University to act with professionalism, giving evidence of competencies and commitment for the desired results.

5)   The actions of University are guided by absolute harmony between speech and action.

6)   It is the duty of the University to work permanently in the construction and improvement of legitimate instruments of education that facilitate the continuous improvement of its target audience.

7)   The precept of the University is to undertake its actions in order to help in preserving and respecting the environment as a condition for the survival of present and future generations.

Concerning organization, the role of the University is based on constant reflection on what should be preserved and what should be changed in search for balance between tradition and renewal, as the basis of education.

In the set of guidelines and principles, UNICO adopts the following actions: (i) to develop an integrated system of education focused on business results; (ii) to instruct for new challenges; (iii) to integrate the entire value chain in the enterprise education effort; (iv) to catalyze and disseminate the culture of the Post Office; (v) to promote citizenship training initiatives; (vi) to allow the continuous improvement of the Company processes; (vii) to use new technologies; (viii) to transform the Postal Museum into a business education tool.

These actions intend to ensure professional development as a strategic element, focusing on results, decentralized management and the auto support through multiple forms of teaching, emphasizing on distance education in educational and technological partnerships.

The educational model at the University Post Office is divided into two large blocks: professional training and increased schooling. Both serve not only the workforce but the entire network of the Company. Its goals are focused on training the employees, raising the brand image of BPTC and facilitate contacts with various partners. The educational model is composed of:

a) Tutorial courses of access and support: they present the business environment in which the post office operates; teaching is done autonomously and by distance learning; they provide introductory notions to the desired course; they allow access to formal education;

b)   New professional training model trains people in various technical and operational procedures; it offers a strategic vision; it transmits culture and corporate values. It gives greater emphasis to distance education;

c)   The increase of schooling serves as the basis for the development of all formal education (with diploma awarded by a higher education institution) that the University offers:

1)   Post-secondary courses: specialization of entry-level staff;

2)   Sequential graduate and extension courses: raising education of technical and higher staff;

3)   Postgraduate for senior staff, including what is called in academic language, *sensu* (master and doctorate) and *broad sense* (specialization, MBA, etc.).

Figure 9 - System Structure of Corporate Education UNICO.

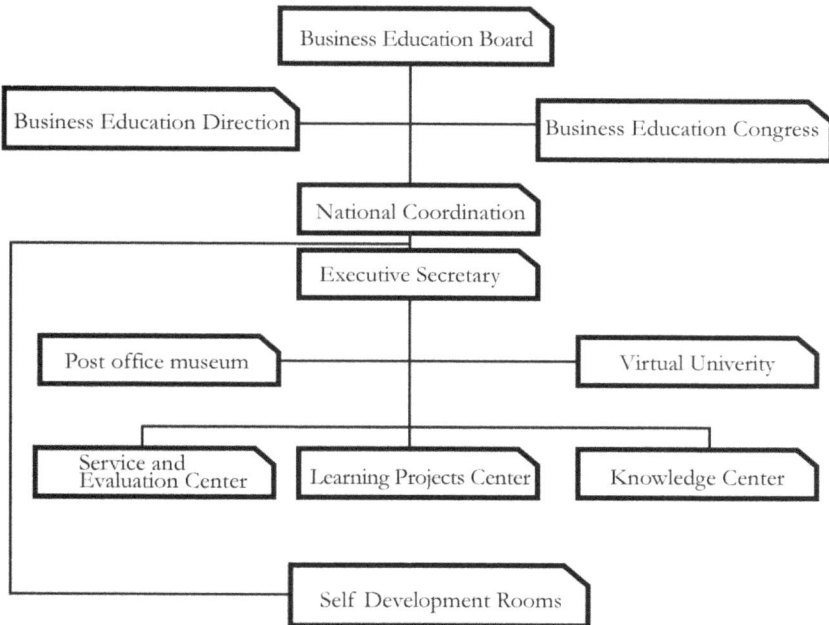

Source: Correios do Brasil website

The figure above shows the structure of corporate education system of the Corporate University of Posts, whose composition is situated in the functions of each area along the educational activities in order to integrate them into business strategies.

a) The Board of Management Education is subordinate to the Board of the Brazilian Post and Telegraph and its functions are: to guide the education system according to the strategic decisions of the Post Office; to approve the National Education Plan; to advise and to assist the Board of Directors in the definition of educational policies and strategies for the company.

b) Policy Management Education has the function of dissemination of institutional values and meet audience needs related to education. Meetings are held every six months to develop their activities.

c) Congress Business Education has the purpose to discuss trends in corporate learning in Brazil and abroad, including the assessment of scientific and technological research work in the postal sector. They meet every two years.

d) National coordination aims to conduct all education activities, national and international, related to the Post value chain, and to represent the link between the Board of Management Education and all corporate educational process.

e) The Executive Secretariat is responsible for all communication, marketing and public relations activities, management of corporate volunteering focused on education, secretarial work of collective bodies, the physical campus janitorial and planning of the University budget. This is part of the structure of the Secretariat Collegiate Agents, the Comptroller and the campus of City Hall.

f) The Post Office Museum is considered the first of the company's knowledge repository. It acts as a center of raw material for the construction and development of business intelligence. It integrates the museum's spaces: booth for selling books and philatelic items, cafeteria / coffee shop, toy library, video library, rooms for implementation of courses and movie theaters.

g) The Virtual University works together with the other agents of the University and it has the virtual campus webmaster function. It is responsible for the secretariat, and it monitors all events offered by the University. In addition, it performs the virtual management of the Library and the Post Office Museum, as well as the Knowledge Communities.

h) The Service Center has the function to search for excellence in the activities of the education system, as well as all segments of the postal value chain. It also carries out evaluation activities of the educational process.

i)   The Learning Projects Center is responsible for all operations planning, production and operation of educational projects. This center is responsible of formatting the courses, lectures, conferences, consulting, research, etc. It is also up to this center the management of infrastructure for classroom educational events at the University.

j)   The Knowing Center has the mission to manage the Company's knowledge bank, offering strategic background information for planning, development and implementation of educational programs. It is the largest repository of the postal chain knowledge.

k)   The Self-Development rooms and Corporate Education Centers, despite their non-physical integration to the campus, determine the specific schedule. It is reserved for activities supporting the development of distance education and open to the community, while its administration is in charge of Regional Divisions.

This chapter deals with a set of six interviews conducted by the researcher with the ROMG managers from the Post office, in accordance with the structured scripts and other unstructured issues that arose during the interviews, but relevant to the subject matter. It was also used, in the document analysis, four editions of the journal "Fala Minas", the internal corporate newsletter of the annual and social report of 2009 and intranet data, which one of the interviewees presented to the researcher, but did not allowed to be copied. To structure the interview scripts, the base organizational theory related to the three topics examined was taken, which theoretical approach presents some evidence of their relationship. The period in which the interviews took place was November 2010 to January 2011, previously scheduled and carried out at the workplace, except for one respondent who preferred to be interviewed at his College where he courses his graduation.

The interviews were recorded with the consent of the respondents, which was emphasized by the researcher at the beginning and end of recordings. As stated in a presentation letter from the researcher to the company, issued by the Office of Graduate Studies and Research, from the Faculdade Novos Horizontes, the confidentiality of the names of the respondents will be remained, naming them through the positions they hold; however, the managers interviewed did not show any concern. Throughout the data collection process, the information through company documents and notes of situations observed at the workplace were also collected.

The average time of the interviews was 30 minutes. There was a significant variation just for two managers interviewed: the operations manager, 19 minutes, and the manager of educational projects, 42 minutes. Regarding the transcripts, they were made by the researcher because it was considered an important step in content analysis, since there is the possibility to realize unidentified elements on the interview of the researched subjects. Subsequently, with all the data on hand, the researcher created a database in *Microsoft Office Word software,* where all the interview transcripts, notes from the observations, photos and scanned images, were grouped and organized according to the specific objectives of the research at the moment. Respondents had the following demographics profile (Table 5):

Table 5 - The profile of respondents.

Position / function	Education	Time on the company	Time on the position	Time on management
Manager of Institutional Relations	Postgraduate Diploma in Strategic Communication	More than 20 years	From 16 to 20 years	More than 20 years
Manager Customer Service	Postgraduate in Retail	More than 20 years	From 16 to 20 years	From 16 to 20 years
Distribution Manager	Postgraduate Diploma in Auditing	From 16 to 20 years	From 11 to 15 years	From 11 to 15 years
Operations Manager	Postgraduate in Human Resources	More than 20 years	More than 20 years	More than 20 years
Commercial Manager	Superior education in Social Communication	More than 20 years	From 11 to 15 years	From 11 to 15 years
Educational Projects Manager	Postgraduate in Education	More than 20 years	From 6 to 10 years	More than 20 years

Source: Research data.

Data were submitted in response to specific goals. This was done due to the large amount of information on different topics, in which evidence of causality between them is sought, allowing thereby a better structuring of data in order to respond more effectively to the objectives that guided this study.

Thus, the organization of presentation and analysis of the data was made as follows: (i) identification of the policies and actions of corporate education; (ii) description of the perception of managers on the existence of the relationship between corporate education and organizational learning; (iii) description of the perception of managers, on the existence of relationship between organizational learning and innovation; and finally, (iv) review, in the perception of managers, of the existence of relationship between corporate education, organizational learning and innovation.

On the previous referential, it is observed that corporate education's mission is the training and development the people who are part of the organization, through knowledge management (generation, assimilation, dissemination and application), and it must be able to generate active and continuous learning. Corporate education becomes more efficient from the use of practices of organizational learning and knowledge management, which it calls as integrating elements of corporate education.

The company researched, according to Official documents (Internal Journal, Internet, Management Report, Social Report, among others) and through interviews, and considers that corporate education is institutionalized education, that aims to prepare men and women to exercise their work in the organization, encompassing four distinct actions: formation, improvement, development and professional training.

Table 6 - Types of actions in Corporate Education.

Types of actions on Corporate Education	Scope	Goals	Time extension	Features
Formation	Prepares and develops the person to practice a profession	wide and mediate	Long term	Qualify for future profession. Taught in schools and even within organizations.
Development and Improvement	Extends and enhances the person to the professional career growth in the organization.	Less broad	Mid-term	It provides knowledge and prepares for complex functions. Given in organizations.
Training	Prepares a person to occupy certain position in the organization and develop particular activity.	Restricted and immediate	Short term	It provides the essential to the current position. Given the organizations or specialized companies.

Source: Adapted from Teixeira (2005 248 p.).

In the context presented above, it is possible to say that the thought of integration of business management to education for work purposes finds its initial motivation in knowing how to do, placed in the context of vocational schools. Although with the introduction of corporate education policies within organizations, another aspect hitherto overlooked in the professional or ideological views (way of being and thinking), has occupied significant space in the current model of corporate education, seeking to develop synergies and merge these two models as a means of developing more effective learning for companies, workers and society.

The operations manager revealed that in his perception, the role of corporate education in the organizational learning process goes beyond the conditions strictly being work-related. There is a company concern with the development of workers as social agents, able to transform the company and the environment in which they live, as their standard of living:

[...] *"In the company, the corporate education, in addition to the task of preparing the person for the job, also prepares as a man, as a human being, it also prepares to live together in society, in addition of course to prepare for their activities, for teamwork."*

This reality seems, in fact, part of the universe of the studied organization. Because, according to the Regional Director of BPTC MG, the importance given to corporate education in the DR/MG made that the Regional branch reached first place in the People Management Index (PMI) , attributing this achievement to overcome in 246, 23% of the target set for training actions and development of employees. Index measured monthly the level of efficiency and quality of services in the area of corporate education. These indicators are endorsed by the Deputy Manager of Educational Actions:

"No one gets to work at the Post Office without first going through the courses with which the person will understand what it is and how the company works.[...] *It is about to participate in the construction of regional Company results, developing and enhancing the knowledge, competencies and attitudes of employees so that they act committed to the business of BPTC, feeling valued and learning to be socially responsible ."*

These elements make emphasis in the speech of managers during the interviews, as they manifest that this understanding is incorporated into the culture of the organization, socialized in the strategic framework by addressing its proposal for organizational development through the actions of corporate education. Thus, it becomes apparent that corporate education, despite their planning and actions concentrated in the Corporate Education Center

(COREC), includes the participation of the entire organizational structure in different time and places, maximizing learning opportunities, which enables the development of competencies necessary for the performance of services provided by BPTC, as advocated in the literature and affirmed by the Management of Institutional Relations."

"Certainly the post office [corporate education] *aims to* empower, develop and form, *because we have some courses that are for training. You are forming a professional. For example, the mailman, you form the mailman. He applies for the job and he still does not know nothing of the activities that he will develop as a mailman. It is after he goes through the course to be mailman. We have also had in the post office the postal technician course. So he is formed, and he have others where people are already in these positions or of higher level helping them to learn even more. So basically, the objectives of corporate education are* to train, develop, empower and train *people. These are courses with more hours and less workload. Each with specific proposal."*

What is clear from the typology of educational actions perceived by managers as those adopted in the company is that the prevailing perception is focused on learning paradigm as the model presented by Meister (1999). In this sense, for the company, there are segments or groups of priority positions for participation in training, qualification, development or formation courses or processes. The Management of Corporate Education states that the courses are prepared according to the organization's needs and in line with the strategic objectives set for the achievement of expected results and targets to be achieved. What exists is the guidance on referral of employees to the educational actions that are most suitable to every need of the teams and people performing certain activity.

"Educational programs are prepared to meet the strategic objectives of the organization. They have specific focuses on work activities performed in each area and for the various functions and to all employees that exist in the company. There is a requirement that all learn and put into practice what is learned. There are courses and training within the company, and outside there are investments on foreign language courses, scholarships for college, all aimed on work developing. When someone participates in the development program, he or she comes back and spreads the results to everyone with who he or she has contact. It is an action in chain, always seeking to achieve the organization's future performance targets."

This is the proposal of BPTC in contemporary times, in which the generation, assimilation, dissemination and application of knowledge are associated with the organization's performance through targets involving the responsibility of all workers and being able to facilitate learning processes and organizational knowledge.

In BPTC, educational programs supplied outside the company offer the following limits for scholarship: 50%, up to the limit of R $ 450.00 for graduation; 50%, up to the limit of R $ 600.00 for Post Graduation; and 80% for language courses, up to the limit of R $ 150.00 reais. In the ROMG, as the year 2010 indicators, 53 scholarships were offered for graduation, with an annual investment of R $ 96,000, 49 scholarships for languages studies with investments of R $ 64,000 and eight postgraduate scholarships with investments of R $ 37 thousand, totaling 110 scholarships out of the company and investments of R $ 197 thousand.

Comparing investments in scholarships offered outside the Corporate University of Post Offices and the Center for Corporate Education - Minas Gerais in relation to profitability results in 2009, the operating income was R $ 159.2 million, the ROMG invested only 0.12% of operating income in educational activities in formal education outside the company. This reveals a trend in companies that structure Corporate Universities to concentrate training and development *in company programs*. This attitude is due to the fact that there is greater flexibility in building curriculum around the desired competencies and training required in processes, improvement, development and training of its workers.

One reason for the emergence of BPTC in the manner as it is today, was the rigidity of formative processes in the classical school (traditional) and the low capacity to meet the needs to train workers to produce goods or services. Thus, when comparing the access numbers to courses offered by COREC-MG and scholarships offered outside the company, the number of jobs offered in the center of corporate education company is much higher than for scholarships offered in other institutions.

Although access to total investments in corporate education have not been disclosed by the company, when comparing the number of scholarships offered in graduate, post graduate and languages, totaling 110 scholarships in the Regional Management of Minas Gerais; in-person courses, training in the workplace (TIW) and distance education (DE), offered by the Corporate Education Center, according to the manager of corporate education, are reaching on average 10,200 monthly participants. There are three probable causes of this educational strategy: first, as previously mentioned, the possibility to adapt the courses to the real needs of the company; the second, the cost in the supply of educational activities outside the organization; and, finally, the obligation required by the national Post Office development plan, each employee must have at least 20 hours of training each month.

> [...] *"The post office has a workload of 20 hours per employee, it is the national plan for the post office. Every employee must have at least 20 hours of training and it should be focused on his activity, for a mailman then the training would be for mailman, if customer service attendant then the training is for this activity, if manager then training is done by the defined area. All this learning agenda is established in order that learning in practice be strengthened."*

Thus, when making the comparison between the number of participants in courses offered in formal education outside the organization, and those offered in the center of corporate education, it has the percentage change between them being less than 0.09% of scholarships to participants in the foreign education system. This business attitude does not represent conclusive results, but only indicators that show the current position of CU's putting together and developing their own educational programs, as really important are the forms of learning, the tuning of the business programs and the inherent temporality in all training process, because it is not enough to identify the required competencies, the use of teaching methods and appropriate learning practices is required.

Note the concern of the CE, BPTC - ROMG, in offering educational programs in order to strengthen the company in the long term and able to meet all its labor force contingent. This concern reaffirms the purposes of corporate education today, inserting the concept of education anytime, anywhere, prepared and tailored to specific situations and objectives to be achieved.

To the interviewed managers, there is a range of evidence that supports this statement because, for them, efforts are being concentrated on facilitating access to workers in the offered courses, regardless of the geographic location in which it is located, as also in courses that provide elements to rethink the practice of work and find ways to facilitate the production of services offered, with the least possible effort to the organization with the development of all partners.

In the long run, there is formation, improvement and training [...]. "There are even training goals in the company. Basically, the workforce is divided into manager and not a manager. Who has an advisory and leadership role, has a learning agenda. *The focus of the competencies to be developed are by department and work area. Who is not manager* is *technical officer occupying its position, and also has a learning agenda. Then for each of these categories, there are training goals that* I *would not know now by heart, but every year a manager and a non manager have to meet certain hours of training."*

And that, in a way, causes people to stay in constant development, that is, thinking in the long run as an uninterrupted development process. Maybe we'll talk forward, but there are several ways, including, in-room and distance education, because a company like ours, and I'm talking in Minas Gerais (MG) level, with 853 counties, one branch in each of them with a post office team in each city, therefore, it is very difficult to move everyone. Because of this we have these two modes, in-room and distance education, so that the knowledge does not stop to be produced or received in any of the points of our structure ."

"It is in the medium and long term, preparing employees and suppliers to perform well their activities and also incorporating new ways of working. In the case of employees, you can see this quite clearly when the company implemented a training policy with minimum workload, this is done in the program to always seek continuous development. When you enter, IT is a type of training you have, then, the training is changing you to become a more complete professional, so that's it, you never stop developing in your role. Today we have several friendly technologies to make it happen, and the Internet and the intranet are the most favorable means. But surely education in the company thinks about today and tomorrow, and I think that's important."

It is observed that the current proposal for corporate education at the Post Office has in its scope the history of the evolutionary process of the T&D model (Training and Development). There T&D was born as a school with more comprehensive proposal for the formation of workers occupying functions requiring higher education. The Superior School of Postal Administration (SSPA) took in its appearance a different posture of the commonly found standards in other companies, establishing in its guidelines the double positioning in its formative process: the business vision and the focus on results, but also, civic education, which thinking was in the man and in the social context in which it appears.

With the establishment of the Corporate University and Corporate Education Centers around the five regions of the country, other actors were covered for the human and organizational development proposal. The value chain participants were integrated into the company's development goals, taking into account that the results when providing the services depend significantly from the *interface* areas that occur between the service provider and customer , strengthening the concept of interface at all stages when providing the service.

 The documents show the company's concern to insert customers in the training process, in view of their participation in the final outcome of the service offered, since it is a broad portfolio of services, with emphasis on corporate clients. It reaffirms that the production efficiency is associated with personalized service and corporate education. In this particular case, it seeks to develop the competencies associated with the role of each actor for the best result of the given or received service.

"When it is talked about corporate university, two parts are involved: university and corporate. University because it is universal, it covers a very wide audience. What audience is this? The audience from corporation, that means, companies. The Corporate University is a study center focused on the interests of the company that reaches a very wide audience with a diversity of somewhat large study . The company's strategic plan is taken and identified what it is needed to be developed. Education is included to complement that plan. And the focus is not only the employees but also the entire company's value chain . Why is there the need to also focus on the value chain? Because it is assumed that the company has an image that is formed not only by its product but also by the employees and all those that add value to the company's services. Are customer, supplier, partners, contractors, etc of the value chain BPTC included? All this audience is reached and covered by the corporate university."

Apparently, the Corporate University was able to reinforce these purposes and extend them throughout the structure of the organization, covering all positions and functions, people and companies that are actually relevant to the outcome of business, in all regions where the company operates. Thus, the BPTC and ROMG, seem to comply with the necessary characteristics to organizations where continuous learning and the ability to manage knowledge are established as differential.

It is necessary that the CE provides learning opportunities aligned to organizational needs as a process and not as physical space, able to hold up on a curriculum that includes the triad of corporate citizenship, contextual structure and basic competencies, and that develops all the chain values and train future workers, which seems to be the purpose of the CE in ROMG.

An example is the "first hour". Once a week, this is reserved for the manager to talk to his team. As the manager explains: "It is an opportunity that we have to report on new developments that are going on now, how to communicate them and also exchange experiences. We inform to the teammates what has been learned back into a course or training, although there are other bases that facilitate this exchange, as the Internet, intranet and distance education platform. So you can see that there are many ways we have and there is no restriction to the classroom or training room."

"There are courses for all the partners. On the site it is possible to find some of them for customers, for companies and staff outsourced in order to prepare all partners, because, to the client, this differentiation does not matter. They are expecting solutions for their businesses."

Generally, in the opinion of managers interviewed, CU encompasses a range of actions directed by well-structured policies that value the productive potential of the company and awaken the workers joint responsibility for the company's results. From this perspective, one can infer that it is a learning company, providing consistency between its institutional proposal of human and corporate development through education, practice and educational activities, according to the perception by managers interviewed.

"Despite the activities that are exclusive [monopoly] from the post office, especially in retail, it is necessary to expand the focus and seek new business opportunities. Today there is concern in expanding the enterprise customer network offering comprehensive and tailored services solutions. While it has a social function, environmental concern, digital security, selective hiring, there are business opportunities, because the company evolves. It is learned where to find the opportunities in which corporate education had a unique role in the organization and dissemination of this knowledge. As one manager said: "Imagine if each learned element were restricted to one place, but the corporate education would play its part, concentrating the knowledge around the organization's objectives and the growth, expansion and motivation outcomes [...]."

It is constant in the speech of managers the concern in offering complete solutions to customers, strengthening the role of the Corporate Education Centers in the expansion of knowledge and learning of employees, suppliers, customers and the company in general because, when meeting the customer needs, the company needs continuous development to understand their desired solutions. This would allow the development of measures that meet and maximize resources, a role that becomes facilitated by corporate education actions and policies .

Individual learning can not be considered organizational learning, but organizational learning can only occur through the subjects that from their work actions, their life experiences, their knowledge acquired from formal education or not, autonomous discoveries, as agent and productive worker, put their knowledge and expertise available to the collective participant in its network of relationships at work. In that availability of individual to the collective knowledge, organizations feed their cognitive and memory systems.

To start this process of knowledge sharing, and enabling to generate learning that not only reaches the employee personally, but teams, sectors and, broadly, throughout the organization, companies must offer satisfactory environmental and technological conditions to the storage of learning and development of new knowledge.

Therefore, the organizational knowledge creation process must be continuous. It is the organization responsibility to promote the proper context for facilitating group activities, as well as the creation and accumulation of knowledge at the individual level.

It is justified the constant interchange between the theories of organizations that address organizational learning and corporate education. Both often assume a complementary role, arguing that the latter is the basis for the first since facilitate to organizations to learn more fluidity and with less effort, achieving better strategic results in consequence.

Organizational learning lies in building blocks of human and organizational development, which takes on different characteristics, but permeated by the systematic attitudes, behaviors, knowledge, competencies and knowledge that add value to the organization. This process can refer to the individual, group, organizational and social learning. Thus, according to the theory, there is convergence between the topics for the parameterization of the concepts around the combination of constituent elements of the relationship between corporate education and organizational learning, being manifested in the speech of respondents:

According to a company manager: "Corporate education came to the company with the future vision of sustainability and improvement of performance. It was a critical period for all businesses, all workers and all companies for the need to reinvent themselves. The end of the 90s was a critical period, and it was in this process that corporate education arrived mapping failures on knowledge and structuring the whole training process. It could not be different. The competition was already installed and even with some areas of monopoly, the company was forced to reinvent its ways on how they delivered their services or they would perish. Not because it is a government company that is sustained if it does not deliver results." [...]

"It was a collective learning because here nobody does anything isolated, all our activities, our processes are interconnected, everything that it's done depends on a very large group of people and knowledge can not focus on people [strategic], because everyone needs to know what has to be done in date and time. Corporate education came to systematize the knowledge in the organization with an intense learning on it. They are courses, training, investments in all worker training areas, and with all this, we were reinventing the ways of doing things. I came to the postal bank due to the characteristic of the company, its presence

in the country, the Sedex (express delivery subsidiary) family grew, it reinvented the telegram, philately changed, the processes and the management have also changed as well."

"This was because the learning was at the heart of all our activities and corporate education was structured so that gave support to all other areas. Corporate education has been preparing people for what they should do well. I see how indistinct factors [...] maybe here you find people who do not share this view, but I think much will confirm this. Among the factors that favor the individual and collective learning are the improvements in employee development. Corporate education opens the possibility of career advancement which means that prepared people have opportunities to move up in the company, increased knowledge and personal and professional development .

As in the literature used as the basis for this study, managers interviewed in the BPTC and ROMG realize that corporate education also has close relationship with organizational learning. To understand the type of relationship established between these two areas of organizational development, it is gathered up the questions so that from the answers could be possible to extract the conceptual understanding of respondents about the meanings of organizational and individual learning attitudes in the company, and the role that corporate education has in the organizational learning process.

When asked to one of the managers on the role of corporate education in the organizational learning process, *"[...] certainly yes, because otherwise not even would be worth for the company to be investing. I think, for example, on improvement courses you can not see 100% of apprehension of what was said, but I think there's a change, people change their behavior and that is what I think learning is. You receive new knowledge and somehow your attitude changes, and so does your behavior. These personal changes also affect those who are close, so there is also organizational learning since teams change their behavior as well. I would not know to tell you how, I could not measure it. I could not tell you how to measure it, but it is noticeable, in practice you realize that a person entered in the company with a certain way of being and today she has a different attitude, a different behavior, commitment. Certainly, there are changes. Changes in the person, changes in the team and changes in the company.*

As shown by the interviewed managers, corporate education in the BPTC, ROMG, brings with it a huge effort to present a corporate educational development proposal guided by learning in the transformation of declarative, explicit knowledge into procedural, tacit knowledge.

"It is about learning with the colleague, work with other sectors. There has been a concern in always improve what people do, so they seek to learn at all, with competitors, with our customers. In the company now people have to constantly improve, so learning must be constant."

"If you want to know about the theoretical knowledge and practical knowledge, both have value in the organization, but here we do not prioritize one over the other. Look, every worker has the knowledge that is received in class, in training courses, but also has practical ones, their work experience, the training offered in the workplace, in connivance with colleagues and this is also taken in consideration , and depending on the activity it performs, it is better for business than theoretical knowledge. But it is clear that I am not saying that theoretical knowledge is of no importance here in the company [...]."

This reinforces the understanding that, for organizational learning and knowledge creation in the company, one needs a proper environment to facilitate group activities, as well as at the individual level. There must be the organization intention, through the aspirations, goals, and autonomy, the permission for all actors to perform in order to introduce unexpected opportunities, working as a holographic structure in which everyone can share information and knowledge, moving from tacit to explicit knowledge .

Modeled on the basis of the knowledge creation process, it is understood that the Post Office, ROMG, corporate education operates at all levels of the process. Initially, one may view the function of corporate education acting as a platform of knowledge creation, as well as sharing and dissemination space throughout the organization, understood as what the theory authors call as *ba*.

There are several actions, for example, the online courses on specific topics, discussion forums on the intranet, the classroom courses assembled according to certain needs, all around the COREC. There is a very large organization for all this to happen according to the company's needs, both in real space and in cyberspace.

Even when there is no clear manifestation on the model understanding in the conversations of respondents, revealing itself in a more empirical way. In the daily organizational needs, this space called *ba* can be viewed with a certain structure. In this sense, it is clear that there is concern on behalf of the company to transform the corporate education centers as a physical, virtual and mental space for the experience sharing through peer contact, established at each workplace, regardless the time or geographic location. These centers would be promoting the conversion of knowledge, competencies and individual attitudes in terms and concepts shared throughout the organization, as long as they reflect on the possibility to improve the organization performance.

According to one of the managers "[...] There is freedom to express what you know or learn; and certainly there are exchanges, expansion of what is known and reflection of what you learned. The company's policy is that there is nothing definitive, everything is evolving and we have to develop, so everything goes through self-development, but also for the development of the teams because no one runs a company alone. While there is freedom to express what you think and what you know, you need to hear and see what others know and think about certain processes, certain activities. I think this corporate education can do well, it brings together all within the company, whatever it does not have, it sought outside and also what it needs to be shared ."

The basis for knowledge conversion lies in sharing and socialization of what is learned in the existential sphere, based on the experience of the subject from his new discoveries stimulated by education initiatives within the company. This enables the reflection with the other actors that are part of their working environment, peers to possibly generate new explicit knowledge and systematize them in specific or related activities, facilitating the transformation of explicit knowledge into tacit, by synthesizing meaningful elements into systematic internalisation in the organization. Therefore, the information gathered in the company, reinforces that the perception of managers is located, although not so structured, in a coherent sequence in the theory discussed along the stages of the process of knowledge creation.

There is evidence that the BPTC company in ROMG, through corporate education, seeks to share the tacit knowledge in a systematic way. For example, in the "first hour", workshops and sharing encouragement of individual and group experiences, create a justified concept, which enables the standardization and guidance deployment to routines and processes throughout the organization-wide scope and the archetype of context. Then, a new value for the company would spread across the enterprise, capable of generating knowledge assets continuously and in accordance with the company's needs. It would also offer solutions to customers based on the changes occurring in the markets in which it operates.

It seems to be more evident to the managers the relationship of corporate education in the BPT and ROMG with organizational learning. Structure converging steps for the creation and dissemination of knowledge and learning are indispensable to the creation of organizational value. This is manifested in the ability that the COREC-MG has to inventory and map the existing organizational knowledge and provide means for the capitalization of new knowledge to drive change to the company operations in the market, or to face them in dynamic and agile way.

Thus, as previously mentioned, Roy Rothwell believes that the current business innovation focuses on capacity that companies have to establish effective relations with the external environment, through alliances, cooperation and integration with others. This external environment should mean in aggregation of value to the product or service offered on the market, but also in the maintenance of cross-functional teams and procurement processes, as well as the sharing of knowledge along the supply chain.

Companies are engaged in innovation due to numerous reasons. Their goals may involve products, markets, efficiency, quality or ability to learn and implement changes. It would identify the reasons that lead companies to innovate, and important assists to examine the forces that drive innovation activities, such as competition and the entry of new market opportunities.

In BPTC, innovation seems to be an inherent condition in the work activity and, in the perception of managers, it focuses on four types of innovation provided by the Oslo Manual: management, products, processes and *marketing*. There is also the understanding that it moves between the poles, radical and incremental. In search of a conceptual understanding of managers, respondents in the areas of operations and distribution share that similar understanding. This can be read on next:

"[...] *Innovation to me is when you do a new thing better, better than is being done now or in the past, or when you do something that nobody has done yet, then you are innovating in a particular activity, service or plan on management.*"

"*[...] The world undergoes a complete revolution in the area of innovation. Be it technology, products, processes, management concept [...] this issue, as its name indicates, is to innovation, changing, and the company is very attentive to what innovation is on the national scene and it seeks to bring into it what really will make a difference. But it is also about the company making a difference, and do it before others do.*"

This understanding is reinforced when the interviewees expressed perceptions of the company's concern to innovate and take the inherent risks in innovation. For them, the most decisive action of innovation in the company is the "Inova Postal" program. In the national competition mode, employees can express their innovative ideas and the top three are implemented in the company, which runs the risks inherent in the innovation process.

Every year through contests, the company opens space for all employees to participate by sending their ideas, according to certain topics related to any necessary solution to the company or customers. This program is widely accepted and has great participation. Throughout the year, employees manifestations are accepted striving to improve the services offered and their production processes.

According to one manager: "The Inova Postal contest is the most obvious space given to innovation in the company, but innovation happens here as necessary solutions to customer demands, manifested by employees, and adaptations from activities that are not of our portfolio. If you think of the Sedex family products, you can see the evolution in the last two decades. Some products of this family have been disabled and others came to meet specific customers needs. There is, yes, an effective pursuit by the company for innovative ideas [...]."

The 2009 year management report devotes an exclusive space to talk about innovation in business. Analyzing the document, the managers´ perception confirms: in the category of radical innovation the winning idea was "Post Office Box with Automatic Confirmation Device on Delivery "launched by the postman, from Nova Serrana.

In services, innovation is the result of an interactive process with customers, suppliers, employees, research centers and others, in which the incremental feature of innovation is most evident. This is the vision that the authors address as consistent with concepts of organizational learning, innovation networks, tacit knowledge and interactive learning.

However, in the sphere of the relationship between organizational learning and innovation in BPT, ROMG, managers seem to view and perceive it, but they are not capable to clearly express how it performs within the enterprise and in the innovation processes. As in the literature addressed in this book, there are nuances of the existence of a relationship, especially as potentiating agent, but without defining characteristics of their participation in the stages of the innovation process.

" It contributes [to Organizational learning] because it is through learning that the employee opens his mind, to new knowledge, to ideas. All this by daily, weekly, monthly learning, exchange of experiences and needs to better serve customers with the help of courses and training. And when he opens his mind to new learning, he opens it to new ways of doing things, it makes room for innovation."

"I do not know how it happens, but in fact it exists. I believe that with learning, the organization becomes more likely to open its world vision, market, quality, customer needs satisfaction, all that through the employees. So if you have people who can see farther, of course they will always reflect on what they do and they will find ways to do better, because I believe this is one of the roles of innovation, since if it is to stay as it is, there is no need to innovate."

On the analysis of several productive sectors, it is concluded that the most impacting condition in organizational learning relationship with the processes of innovation depends on specific organizational contexts and it is associated with technological characteristics, environments and company guidance for learning, value of innovation to the company's *performance* and the potential of their human assets.

Thus, in the BPTC, these characteristics are favorable so there is a collaborative and empowered active relationship between relational aspects of research. It is necessary to understand that education becomes an important element for organizational learning, as evidenced by the perception of managers. However, the evidence that organizational learning and corporate education are able to encourage innovation in the company are not clearly expressed. There is no structure for operating the interference process.

The proposal combined on the theory used in this study addresses this issue as a virtuous circle, constantly moving, in which the corporate education promotes organizational learning, and emphasized by managers of the BPTC. Organizational learning leads to innovation, which requires new learning from the organization, which responsibility for planning and executing these actions would be of corporate education. However, this relationship is not so clear for managers who fail to manifest it in a structured thought sequence.

The organization constantly undergoes through changes and amendments by a process including innovation. What is learned as innovation , certainly comes from organizational learning, the training of these people in the company, and the customer who also helps in innovation . For example, the customers require quality products and in a way to meet their needs. All this shows that innovation is a need to better serve the customer.

"You can fully assert , because I can not explain how, but clearly there is such relationship, but in fact I can not explain how this is so interconnected, according to what you ask. You can not deny that organizational learning is an evolving process, and that corporate education has transformed the company in its knowledge and learning, so therefore the relationship with innovation. But in a sequenced effect, it might not be as linked as you think."

Thus, it is undeniable the company's positioning for innovation, however it was not possible to measure it on its relations levels with corporate education and organizational learning.

The thematic triad discussion and analysis of organizational studies, corporate education, organizational learning and business innovation, are addressed in several business sectors and in many productive sectors by the academy. This is due to the importance of each one of them on organizational development and performance of companies. In practice, within organizations, the concern on structuring each of these enhancer *performance systems* is relevant , in which the three have outstanding importance in this scenario of constant change.

In BPTC, ROMG, this interest is not different. The company offers a broad portfolio of products and services as well as an ongoing business development. The company stands out for its public trust and credibility for the services provided to clients, which includes of all kinds, inserted in the totality of its mission: "to provide affordable and reliable solutions to connect people, institutions and businesses in Brazil and in the world ".

Thus, the corporate education in the BPTC, since 2001, has won more consistent contours with the theoretical proposal presented by the principal authors of this work. Thus, as perceived by respondents actors, managers, these actions significantly reflect how the organization learns and especially how organizational knowledge is generated and disseminated within the organization.

For managers, corporate education adds value to the organization development capacity when compared to the creation of organizational knowledge model, which can only occur through people who compose it. So the existence of an educational system in line with the organization strategic objectives can rely on each worker and their competencies to develop them effectively.

Corporate Education (CE), with its policies and actions, favors organizational learning (OL) and the organizational knowledge management (OK) by strengthening the necessary spaces, whether the workplace as a space for learning, the classrooms as spaces for production and appropriation of knowledge and expertise. This expands the epistemological and ontological vision of knowledge in people, allowing the understanding that the very existence of every worker in their professional memorial should be a tool for the identification, production, assimilation, dissemination, integration and modification of knowledge, in addition to enable a wider sphere reflecting moderating element that at the same time can be considered the *Ba*.

Corporate education also favors that shared space, allowing fluidity of that knowledge and learning that is inherent in the existence of individuals, peers and organization, returning in a new process.

The set of values and guidelines presented by the CE in BPTC-ROMG influence in the creation and conversion of knowledge in which the SECI model is enhanced in its own process of transformation of conceptual knowledge elements on a conversion movement to the operationalization of those concepts in practice. All this reflects the construction of a learning agenda to map the needed knowledge to positions and functions within the organization. Whereas in the absence of constituent elements of such learning, the COREC is responsible for finding ways to support the company in these *gaps* using - whether internal or external- resources.

Thereby, when building up the assets of knowledge, participants give feedback about the converting base and creation of knowledge generators of organizational learning, converted into experiential , conceptual, systemic and habitual or routinized contexts. Thus, the second specific objective of this study can be answered, as there is in the perception of managers, the relationship of encouragement, strengthening and fostering organizational learning through corporate education.

On the third goal, the analyzed material indicates that there is a relationship between corporate education and organizational learning with innovation in BPTC- ROMG. It is characterized as an innovative company, since it has the typical and necessary characteristics and elements for this statement . When forms of relationship are analyzed , in managers' speeches and analyzed documents show nuances that there are positive interference in the innovation process, but managers can not establish the way it precisely happens.

> "[...] *We believe that both function as a cycle, reaching to innovation. Education serves to broaden our view on an issue or knowledge, then from the provided learning by the corporate education the company is more able to innovate.*

This speech, like the others, reinforce the lack of structure in the interference mode on innovation. Even with a set of products and services that have suffered or are suffering some either radical or incremental innovation, managers can not establish a causal relationship. Interference manifests itself more clearly by the competition pressure caused , than necessarily by learning efforts.

"[...] *There have been several social responsibility initiatives that may become a new business niche. You can see in our branches the battery recycling bins, we are innovating in our services, but the legislation will require companies to do reverse logistics, this will be a business opportunity, as well as Braille postal services or answering in sign language, that brings new customers and new opportunities [...]*.

Figure 10 - Perceived Relationship For Managers.

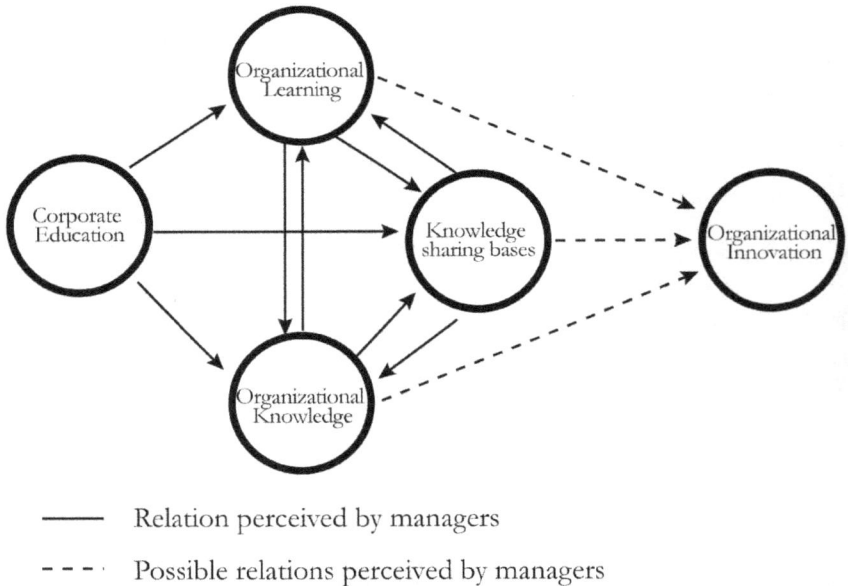

——— Relation perceived by managers

- - - Possible relations perceived by managers

Source: Research Data.

Thus, the above figure is the possible contributive relation of corporate education, learning and organizational knowledge for innovation in the company; however, this association does not manifest itself clearly in the responses of managers for their concrete existence.

CHAPTER 9
FINAL CONSIDERATIONS

This descriptive study aimed to investigate the perception of managers, the existence of relationship between corporate education, organizational learning and business innovation. For this, the field research was applied to the Post and Telegraph Company, Regional Director of Minas Gerais (PTC-ROMG), using a qualitative approach.

This choice is due to the search for non-quantifiable nuances converging to the research objectives. A systematic review of the literature led to propositions on the theme that revealed the existence of relationship between the themes addressed; however, none of the cited authors show clarity about the process of interference *associated with the mapped interdependence and significant evidence on a contingency structure.*

In this context, the first specific objective aims to evaluate the corporate education policies and actions taken by the studied company , considering the sector in which it operates: the provision of services. This aspect needs to be emphasized because, due to the characteristics of the service as of intangibility, indivisibility, variability, and perishability, it results in a different educational action from that used by other productive sectors. It combines the variation between production efficiency *versus* opportunities, given the variations in the areas of contact between provider and recipient. These are divided into damped operations, permeable and reactive system, depending on the degree of contact with the customer and the requirements for the work activity with a focus on operations, since the production in critical areas of interaction demand greater customization.

A developmental scenario was found in the area of corporate education, focused on the expansion of learning, and human and organizational knowledge, which includes in its sphere of action the following: customers, suppliers, employees and other partners of the institution, being in customized programs. In BPTC, ROMG, educational programs are developed based on the specific needs of the organization and flexibility in form and content, and the adjustment to organizational strategies and competencies development.

These findings show up to be productive for the post office, in the achievement of the company's strategic purposes. However, when considering the emancipatory dimension that the educational activity has over the individual agent on the educational act, there are limitations from the features that this action develops in the subject. They are concentrated in the labor act and present themselves with limiting coverage on reflective and autonomous actions, since each employee is a participant in a process that includes, himself and his purpose in education actions.

This dimension of education can then be enhanced by examining the perception of managers, revealing that the main purpose of corporate education in the BPTC, ROMG, is to develop the workforce according to the needs of each performed activity, and taking advantage in the market in which it operates. Therefore the whole time period of the employee within the organization is conducive to the development of new competencies, knowledge, attitudes and values. For managers, there is the strengthening of the concept that development not only is located in areas as the workplace. It could also be the home, where the employee can access a course *on line,* enabling the expansion of learning opportunities .

This leads workers to changes in their behavior and commit to their development at work. For its development in the company, in the sense of progression, the requirements are established around the contribution of knowledge and individual learning and group work, but reveals that educational action focuses its efforts in the labor act and not the subject of the work. The concept of corporate education in the researched company is based on the expansion of individual learning models for strengthening organizational learning, resulting in arising knowledge and learning maps from desired or expected competencies inventories and those perceived as necessary for the company.

Thus, when the second specific goal is addressed , it is observed that corporate education has a relation with the processes of learning and organizational knowledge: from the application of educational activities divided into four focus areas - training, development, improvement and formation- through which the learning and knowledge is generated, disseminated and expanded in micro and macro organizational context. The less embracing conjuncture are the learning and knowledge acquired by acting subjects in the company, located in this definition as *stakeholders;* and the most embracing is the current and recorded knowledge in the organization memory.

Thus, the educational action concentrates efforts on production and organization of the individual learning that could result in productive performance for the company, as long as all the learning and knowledge generated begin to be incorporated as organization assets .

The way in which the third specific objective of this study is approached is through the perception of managers regarding corporate education and organizational learning with innovation processes. It is perceived more incremental than radically, and with less density. Nevertheless, the company is considered innovative to the managers interviewed and converges with the above literature, but it was not possible to identify the direction of the interference of corporate education and organizational learning for this particular purpose.

For a clearer identification of this relationship, it was necessary that managers expressed the educational activities and learned knowledge with specific focus on innovation and the results for both. Thus, there is evidence that the company encourages innovation, but not necessarily through corporate education and organizational learning, unconscious of a consequence, since the perceptions expressed reinforce the sense that both are situated more in the field of organizational performance rather than in innovation. This only reinforces the company's concern in adding value to products or services offered to customers, but not the effective guidance for innovation through learning and knowledge previously established as necessary to this effect.

It is considered that, in the Brazilian Posts and Telegraphs Company, at the ROMG, corporate education acts positively on learning and organizational knowledge, establishing bridges between wisdom and personal knowledge and those external to the organization, adding value to the company, developing personal competencies that imply learning also for the organization.

But this relationship is not stated for innovation in the company, as it has been mentioned on the last specific objective of this work.

Limitations of this book are related to the kind of research and the means used, for example the case study, which does not allow generalizations. Thus, because it is a regionalized study, other regional offices can have different identified results, given the limited research context.

Another hindering point to be considered is the fact that only managers were interviewed, not including other actors as research subjects. This limits the data collection and the information used for the analysis of the research. However, at least in part, this limitation can be compensated with other sources of information, such as documents and observation.

It is also understood that the survey data could expand the researcher's field vision for more comprehensive analysis if the qualitative approach had established confrontation with the quantitative approach through methodological triangulation. It is understandable, therefore, that there would be more questions and possible reflections to be addressed in this work, expanding the scope and density of the assessments made in the considerations.

Based on the analysis of the data and the limitations of this book, it is suggested for future work, from the perspective of descriptive research:

a) Replication in other service organizations, in both the public sector and the private sector, of different sizes and regions;

b) The use of methodological triangulation, covering a larger group of organizational actors in positions and diverse functions;

c) The construction of an array of cause and effect, to measure the expected results, perceived and occurred.

Finally, it is considered that, with the results obtained, the objectives were achieved. Nevertheless, it is emphasized that there was no intention to exhaust the addressed topic , even because it is a study that includes a significant number of elements whose action has ambiguity in the context of inter-relationships or lack of relationships between them. It is expected that this book contributes to the reflection and discussion in the academia and industry.

REFERENCES

ANTAL, Ariane Berthoin et al. Introdution: finding paths through the handbook. In: DIERKES, Meinolf et al. (Editors). Handbook of organizational learning and knowledge. New York: Oxford press, 2001.

ANTONACOPOULOU, Elena. Desenvolvendo gerentes aprendizes dentro de organizações de aprendizagem: o caso de três grandes bancos varejistas. In: EASTERBY-SMITH, Mark; BURGOYNE, John; ARAUJO, Luis. Aprendizagem organizacional e organização da aprendizagem: desenvolvimento na teoria e na prática. Tradução: Sylvia Maria Azevedo Roesch. São Paulo: Atlas, 2001.

ARGYRIS, C.; SCHÖN, D. A. Organizational learning: a theory in action perspecctive. Reading, MA: Addison-Wesley, 1978.

BARBIERE, José Carlos. Organizações inovadoras: estudos e casos brasileiros. Rio de Janeiro: FGV, 2003.

BARRY, Wylant. Design thinking and the experience of innovation. Design issues, Spring, v. 24, p. 3-14, 2008.

BAYMA, Fátima. Educação Corporativa: desenvolvendo e gerenciando competências (Org.). São Paulo: Pearson Prentice Hall, 2004.

AYAS, Karen. Estruturação de projetos para a aprendizagem e a inovação: lições com a pesquisa-ação em uma companhia manufatureira de aeronaves. In: EASTERBY-SMITH, Mark; BURGOYNE, John; ARAUJO, Luis. Aprendizagem organizacional e organização da aprendizagem: desenvolvimento na teoria e na prática. Tradução: Sylvia Maria Azevedo Roesch. São Paulo: Atlas, 2001.

BERTUCCI, Janete Lara de Oliveira. Ambiente, estratégia e performance organizacional no setor industrial e de serviços. Revista de Administração de Empresas – RAE, São Paulo, v. 45, n. 3, p. 10-24, Julho/setembro, 2005.

BESANKO, David et al. A economia da estratégia. Tradução: B. Tecnologia e linguística. São Paulo: Bookman, 2005.

BITENCOURT, Cláudia Cristina; SOUZA, Yeda Swirski. Das práticas de aprendizagem a aprendizagem organizacional. In: Encontro Anual da Associação dos Programas de Pós-Graduação em Administração - EnANPAD, 2003. Anais... Atibaia: ANPAD, 2003.

BRITO, Eliane Pereira Zamith; BRITO, Luiz Artur Ledur; MORGANTI, Fábio. Inovação e o desempenho empresarial: lucro ou crescimento? RAE-eletrônica, v. 8, n. 1, Art. 6, jan/jun 2009. Disponível em: <http://www.rae.com.br/eletronica/ index.cfm?FuseAction=Artigo&ID=5232&Secao=

ARTIGOS&Volume=8&Numero=1&Ano=2009>. Acesso em: 21 maio 2010.

BURREL, Gibson. Ciência normal, paradigmas, metáforas, discursos e genealogia da análise. In: CLEGG, S. R.; HARDY, C.; NORD, W. R. (Orgs.) & FACHIN, R., FISCHER, T. (Orgs. ed. bras.). Handbook de estudos organizacionais. São Paulo: Atlas, 1998. Volume I.

CARRIERI, Alexandre de P.; LUZ, Talita R. Paradigmas e Metodologias: não existe pecado do lado de baixo do equador. In: Encontro Anual da Associação dos Programas de Pós-Graduação em Administração - EnANPAD, 1998. Anais... Foz do Iguaçu: ANPAD, 1998.

CASTELLS, Manuel. Sociedade em rede. São Paulo: Paz e Terra, 1999.

COHEN, Wesley M.; LEVINTHAL, Daniel A. Absorptive Capacity: A new perspective on learning and innovation. Administrative Science Quarteriy, n. 35, p. 128-152, 1990.

CORREIOS. Relatório Social 2009. Diretoria Regional de Minas Gerais, 2009.

CORREIOS. Relatório de Gestão 2009. Diretoria Regional de Minas Gerais, 2009.

DADOY, Mireille. As noções de competência e competências à luz das transformações na gestão da mão-de-obra. In: TOMASI, Antônio (Org.). Da qualificação a competência: pensando o século XXI. Campinas: Papirus, 2004.

DECRETO-LEI Nº 509, de 20 de março de 1969. Publicado no D. O. U. 21.3.1969.

DAVEL, Eduardo; MELO, Marlene Catarina de Oliveira Lopes (Orgs.). Gerência em ação: singularidades e dilemas do trabalho dos gerentes. Rio de Janeiro: FGV, 2005.

DE MASI, Domenico. A Sociedade pós-industrial. São Paulo: SENAC, 1999.

DIBELLA, Anthony J.; NEVIS, Edwin C. Como as organizações aprendem: uma estratégia integrada voltada para a construção da capacidade de aprendizagem. Tradução: Flávio Kuczynski. São Paulo: Educator, 1999.

DINSMORE, Paul Campbell (Org). TEAL – Treinamento experiencial ao ar livre: uma revolução em educação empresarial. Rio de Janeiro: SENAC/ Rio, 2004.

DOWBOR, Ladislau. O que acontece com o trabalho. São Paulo: SENAC, 2001.

DRUCKER, Peter. O melhor de Peter Drucker: o homem. Tradução: Maria Lúcia L. Rosa. São Paulo: Nobel, 2001a.

DRUCKER, Peter. O melhor de Peter Drucker: a administração. Tradução: Arlete Simille Marques. São Paulo: Nobel, 2001b.

DRUCKER, Peter; NAKAUCHI, Isao. Drucker na Ásia: um diálogo envolvente entre Peter Drucker e um dos maiores empresários do Japão. São Paulo: Pioneira, 1997.

EASTERBY-SMITH, Mark; ARAUJO, Luis. Aprendizagem organizacional: oportunidades e debates atuais. In: EASTERBY-SMITH, Mark; BURGOYNE, John; ARAUJO, Luis. Aprendizagem organizacional e organização da aprendizagem: desenvolvimento na teoria e na prática. Tradução: Sylvia Maria Azevedo Roesch. São Paulo: Atlas, 2001.

EASTERBY-SMITH, Mark; BURGOYNE, John; ARAUJO, Luis. Aprendizagem organizacional e organização da aprendizagem: desenvolvimento na teoria e na prática. Tradução: Sylvia Maria Azevedo Roesch. São Paulo: Atlas, 2001.

EBOLI, Marisa. Coletânea universidades corporativas: educação para empresas do século XXI (Coord.). São Paulo: Schmukler Editores, 1999.

EBOLI, Marisa. O desenvolvimento das pessoas e a educação corporativa. In: FLEURY, Maria Tereza Leme (Coord.). As pessoas na organização. São Paulo: Gente, 2002.

EBOLI, Marisa. Educação Corporativa no Brasil: mitos e verdades. São Paulo: Gente, 2004.

FALA MINAS. Revista da Empresa de Correios e Telégrafos – Diretoria de Minas Gerais. Junho, 2009.

FALA MINAS. Revista da Empresa de Correios e Telégrafos – Diretoria de Minas Gerais. Agosto, 2009.

FALA MINAS. Revista da Empresa de Correios e Telégrafos – Diretoria de Minas Gerais. Outubro, 2009.

FALA MINAS. Revista da Empresa de Correios e Telégrafos – Diretoria de Minas Gerais. Novembro, 2009.

FIOL, C. Marlena; LYLES, Marjorie A. Organizational Learning. Academy of Management Review, vol. 10, n. 4, p. 803-8013, 1985.

FIDALGO, Nara Luciene R; FIDALGO, Fernando Selmar R. A lógica de competências e a certificação profissional. In: ARANHA, Antonia Vitória S.; CUNHA, Daisy Moreira; LAUDARES, João Bosco (Orgs.). Diálogos sobre o trabalho: perspectivas multidisciplinares. Campinas: Papirus, 2005.

FINGER, Matthias; BRAND, Silvia Burgin. Conceitos de Organização de Aprendizagem aplicado à transformação do setor público: contribuições conceituais ao desenvolvimento da teoria. In: EASTERBY-SMITH, Mark; BURGOYNE, John; ARAUJO, Luis. Aprendizagem organizacional e organização da aprendizagem: desenvolvimento na teoria e na prática. Tradução: Sylvia Maria Azevedo Roesch. São Paulo: Atlas, ano 2001.

FLEURY, Maria Tereza Leme. As pessoas na organização. São Paulo: Gente, 2002.

FLEURY, Afonso Carlos Correia; FLEURY, Maria Tereza Leme. Estratégias empresariais e formação de competências: um quebra cabeça caleidoscópio da indústria brasileira. Rio de janeiro: Atlas, 2001.

FINEP - FINANCIADORA DE ESTUDOS E PROJETOS. Manual de Oslo: proposta de diretrizes para a coleta e interpretação de dados sobre a inovação tecnológica. 2006. Tradução oficial realizada pela FINEP/Brasil, baseada na versão original da OECD (2005).

FINGER, Matthias; BRAND, Silvia Burgin. Conceitos de Organização de Aprendizagem aplicado à transformação do setor público: contribuições conceituais ao desenvolvimento da teoria. In: EASTERBY-SMITH, Mark; BURGOYNE, John; ARAUJO, Luis. Aprendizagem organizacional e organização da aprendizagem: desenvolvimento na teoria e na prática. Tradução: Sylvia Maria Azevedo Roesch. São Paulo: Atlas, ano 2001.

FLIKKEMA, Meindert J.; JANSEN, Paul. G. W.; SLUIS, Lidewey van der. Identifying Neo-Schumpeterian Innovation in Service Firms: A Conceptual Essay with a Novel Classification. Economics of Innovation and New Technology, n. 16 v. 7, pp. 541-558, 2007.

FITZSIMMONS, James A.; FITZSIMMONS, Mona. Administração de serviços: operação, estratégia e tecnologia de informação. 2. ed. Tradução: Gustavo Severo de Borba et al. Porto Alegre: Bookman, 2000.

FREIRE, Paulo. Educação e mudança. Rio de Janeiro: Paz e Terra, 1979.

GALLOUJ, Faïz. Economia da Inovação: um balanço dos debates recentes. In: BERNARDES, Roberto; ANDREASS, Tales. Inovação em serviços intensivos em conhecimento. São Paulo: Saraiva, 2007.

GOMES, Paulo Alcântara. Uma visão estratégica da educação corporativa. In: BAYMA, Fátima. (Org.). Educação Corporativa: desenvolvendo e gerenciando competências. São Paulo: Pearson Prentice Hall, 2004.

GOMES, Giancarlos; MACHADO, Denise Del Pra Netto; GIOTTO, Olívio Tiago. Análise do conteúdo dos artigos de inovação publicados nos anais do ALTEC, SIMPOI e ENANPAD (2003-2007). SIMPOI – Simpósio de administração da produção, logística e operações internacionais. Anais... São Paulo, 2009.

GOPALAKRISHNAN, Shanthi. Unraveling the links between dimensions of innovation and organizational performance. The journal of high technology management research, v. 1, n. 1, p. 137-153, 2000.

GRINSPUN, Mírian P. S. Zippin. Educação tecnológica. In: GRINSPUN, Mírian P. S. Zippin (Org.). Educação tecnológica: desafios e perspectivas. São Paulo: Cortez, 2002.

HAMDANI, Daood. Serviços, criação de conhecimento e inovação. In: BERNARDES, R.; ANDREASS, T. Inovação em serviços intensivos em conhecimento. São Paulo: Saraiva, 2007.

HANNAN, Michael T.; FREEMAN, John. The population ecology of organizations. American Journal of sociology, v. 82, n. 5, p. 929-964, 1977.

HELAL, Diogo Henrique; LINS, Silze Anne Gonçalves; OLIVEIRA, Rezilda Rodrigues. A institucionalização do modelo de competência: o caso SENAC/PE. In: HELAL, Diogo Henrique; GARCIA, Fernando Coutinho; HONÓRIO, Luiz Carlos. Gestão de pessoas e competências: teoria e pesquisa. Curitiba: Juruá, 2008.

HUERTAS, Melby Karina Zuniga et al. Inovação e marketing em serviços – conceitos e práticas. In: BERNARDES, Roberto; ANDREASS, Tales. Inovação em serviços intensivos em conhecimento. São Paulo: Saraiva, 2007.

HUMES, Leila Lage et al. Treinamento e Capacitação. In: MARQUES, Gil da Costa; CARVALHO, Tereza Cristina M. B. Planejamento estratégico para TI na USP. São Paulo: USP, Livraria da Física, 2007.

HUYSMAN, Marleen. Contrabalançando Tendências: uma revisão crítica da literatura sobre a aprendizagem organizacional. In: EASTERBY-SMITH, Mark; BURGOYNE, John; ARAUJO, Luis. Aprendizagem organizacional e organização da aprendizagem: desenvolvimento na teoria e na prática. Tradução: Sylvia Maria Azevedo Roesch. São Paulo: Atlas, 2001.

JOHNSON, Gerry; SCHOLES, Kevan; WHITTINGTON, Richard. Explorando a estratégia corporativa: textos e casos. 7. ed. Tradução: Luciana de Oliveira da Rocha. Porto Alegre: Bookman, 2007.

KLERING, Luis Roque; ANDRADE, Jackeline Amantino. Inovação na gestão pública: compreensão do conceito a partir da teoria e da prática. In: JACOBI, Pedro; PINHO, José Antônio. Inovação no campo da gestão pública local: novos desafios novos patamares. Rio de Janeiro: FGV, 2006.

KUBOTA, Luis Cláudio. A inovação tecnológica das firmas de serviço no Brasil. In: DE NIGRE, João Alberto; KUBOTA, Luis Cláudio (Orgs.). Estrutura e dinâmica do setor de serviços no Brasil. Brasília: IPEA, 2006.

KOTLER, Philip. Marketing de serviços profissionais. 2. ed. Barueri, SP: Manole, 2002.

LEI Nº 6.538/78, de 22 de junho de 1978. Publicado no D. O. U. 23.06.1978.

LEMOS, Cristina. Inovação na era do conhecimento. In: LASTRES, Helena M. M.; ALBAGLI, Sarita (Orgs.). Informação e globalização na era do conhecimento. Rio de Janeiro: Campus, 1999.

LIMA, Cássia Helena Pereira; VIEIRA, Adriane. Do Sacrifício ao Sacro Ofício: um modelo para a compreensão do significado do trabalho. In: GOULART, Íris Barbosa (Org.). Temas de psicologia e administração. São Paulo: Casa do Psicólogo, 2006.

LUDKE, Menga; ANDRÉ, Marli E. D. Pesquisa em educação: abordagens qualitativas. São Paulo: EPU, 1986.

MARKERT, Werner. Trabalho, comunicação e competência. Campinas: Autores Associados, 2004.

MARQUARDT, Michael J. O poder da aprendizagem pela ação: como solucionar problemas e desenvolver líderes em tempo real. Tradução: Anna Lobo. Rio de Janeiro: SENAC-RIO, 2005.

MAY, Matthew E. The elegant solution: toyota's formula for mastering innovation. Simon and Schuster: New York, 2007.

MEISTER, Jeanne C. Educação Corporativa. São Paulo: MAKRON Books, 1999.

MILES, Ian. Serviços e Inovação na Europa. In: BERNARDES, Roberto; ANDREASS, Tales. Inovação em serviços intensivos em conhecimento. São Paulo: Saraiva, 2007.

MINTZBERG, Henry; AHLSTRAND, Bruce; LAMPEL, Joseph. Safári de estratégia: um roteiro pela selva do planejamento estratégico. Tradução: Nivaldo Montingelli Jr. Porto alegre: Bookman, 2000.

MINTZBERG, Henry. Moldando a estratégia. In: MINTZBERG, Henry et al. O processo da estratégia: conceitos, contextos e casos selecionados. Tradução: Luciana de Oliveira da Rocha. Porto alegre: Bookman, 2006.

MINTZBERG, Henry et al. O processo da estratégia: conceitos, contextos e casos selecionados. Tradução: Luciana de Oliveira da Rocha. Porto alegre: Bookman, 2006.

MORGAN, Gareth. Paradigmas, metáforas e resolução de quebra-cabeças na teoria das organizações. RAE - Revista de Administração de Empresas, São Paulo, v. 45, n. 01, p. 58-71, Jan/Mar. 2005.

MOTTA, Fernando C. P.; VASCONCELOS, Isabella. F. G. Teoria Geral da Administração. São Paulo: Pioneira Thomson Learning, 2004.

MUSSAK, Eugenio. Metacompetência: uma nova visão do trabalho e da realização pessoal. São Paulo: Gente, 2003.

MUNDIM, Ana Paula Freitas. Desenvolvimento de produtos e educação corporativa. São Paulo: Atlas, 2002.

NONAKA, Ikujiro; KONNO, Noburo. The Concept of "Ba": Building a Foundation for Knowledge Creation. California Management Review, v. 40, n. 3, spring, 1998.

NONAKA, Ikujiro. A empresa criadora de conhecimento. In: Harvard Business Review. Gestão do Conhecimento/ Harvard Business Review. Tradução: Afonso Celso da Cunha Serra. Rio de Janeiro: Elsevier, 2000.

NONAKA, Ikujiro; RYOKO, Toyama; BYOSIÈRE, Philippe. A theory of organizational knowledge creation: understanding the dynamic process of creating knowledge. In: DIERKES, Meinolf et al. (Editors). Handbook of organizational learning and knowledge. New York: Oxford press, 2001.

OLIVEIRA, Márcia Regina; SANTOS, Isabel Cristina; LOURENÇÃO, Paulo Tadeu de Mello. Avaliação por competência em ambientes de alta tecnologia. In: CHAMON, Edna Maria Q. O. (Org.). Gestão integrada de Organizações. Rio de Janeiro: Brasport, 2008.

OLIVEIRA, José Maria et al. Universidade Corporativa: o caso de uma estatal estudado à luz do modelo de Meister. In: Simpósio de Excelência em Gestão e Tecnologia – SEGeT, V.Anais... Rio de Janeiro, 2008.

PATON, Rob; PETERS, Geoff; STOREY, John; TAYLOR, Scott. Handbook Corporate University Development: Managing strategic learning initiatives in public and private domains. London: Gower, 2005.

PAWLOWSKY, Peter. The treatment of organizational learning in management science. In: DIERKES, Meinolf et al. (Editors). Handbook of organizational learning and knowledge. New York: Oxford press, 2001.

PAWLOWSKY, Peter; FORSLIN, Jan; REINHARDT. Practices and tools of organizational learning. In: DIERKES, Meinolf et al. (Editors). Handbook of organizational learning and knowledge. New York: Oxford press, 2001.

PORTELLA, Eduardo. Educação, comunicação, saber. In: BAYMA, Fátima. (Org.). Educação Corporativa: desenvolvendo e gerenciando competências. São Paulo: Pearson Prentice Hall, 2004.

PRANGE, Christiane. Aprendizagem Organizacional: desesperadamente em busca de teorias? In: EASTERBY-SMITH, Mark; BURGOYNE, John; ARAUJO, Luis. Aprendizagem organizacional e organização da aprendizagem: desenvolvimento na teoria e na prática. Tradução: Sylvia Maria Azevedo Roesch. São Paulo: Atlas, 2001.

PROKOPENKO, Joseph. Management development: a guide for the profession. Geneva: International Labour office, 1998.

ROTHWELL, Roy. Industrial innovation: success, strategy, trends.In: DODGSON, M.; ROTHWELL, R (Eds.) The handbook of industrial innovation. Hants: Edward Elgar, 1994.

SAVIANI, Demerval. O trabalho como princípio educativo frente às novas tecnologias. In: FERRETTI, Celso João; ZIBAS, Dagmar M. L.; MADEIRA, Felícia R.; FRANCO, Maria Laura P. B. (Orgs.), Novas tecnologias, trabalho e educação: um debate multidisciplinar. Petrópolis: Vozes, 1994.

SARDAN, J-P. O. Anthropologie et dévelopment: Essai en socio-anthropologie du changement social. Paris: APAD-Karthaela, 1995.

SCHUMPETER, Joseph. The Creative Response in Economic History. In: Essays on Entrepreneurs, Innovations, Business Cycles, and the Evolution of Capitalism, Richard V. Clemence, ed. (Piscataway, NJ: Transaction Publishers, 1989): p. 221–224.

SENGE, Peter M. A quinta disciplina: arte, teoria e prática da organização de aprendizagem. 7. ed. São Paulo: Best Seller, 1990.

SBRAGIA, Roberto; KRUGLIANKAS, Isak; ARANGO-ALZATE, Tatiana. Empresas inovadoras no Brasil: uma proposição de tipologia e características associadas. São Paulo: PGT/FEA-FIA/USP, 1999.

SCHWARTZ, Yves. Trabalho e saber. Revista Trabalho e Educação, Belo Horizonte, v. 12, n. 1, p. 21-34, jan./jun. 2003.

STEWART, Thomas A. A riqueza do conhecimento: o capital intelectual e a organização do século XXI. Tradução: Afonso Celso da Cunha Serra. Rio de Janeiro: Campus, 2002.

TARAPANOFF, Kira. Panorama da educação corporativa no com texto internacional. In: Secretária de Tecnologia Industrial (Org.). Educação corporativa: contribuição para a competitividade Brasília: Petróleo Brasileiro e CNI, 2004.

TOFFLER, Alvin. A terceira onda. Tradução de João Távara. 16. ed. Rio de Janeiro: Record, 1980.

TOURAINE, Alain. Um novo paradigma: para compreender o mundo de hoje. Tradução de Gentil Avelino Titton. 3. ed. Petrópolis, RJ: Vozes, 2007.

VAN WIJK, Raymond; VAN DEN BOSCH; Frans A. J; VOLBERDA, Henk W. Knowledge and networks. In: ESTERBY-SMITH, Mark and LYLES; Marjorie A. (Editors). The Blackwell handbook of organizational learning and knowledge management. United Kingdom: MPG books, 2003.

ZARIFIAN, Philippe. Objetivo competência. São Paulo: Atlas, 2001.

ZUBOFF, S. In the age of the smart machine the feature of work and power. New York: Basic Book, 1988.

www.ingramcontent.com/pod-product-compliance
Lightning Source LLC
Chambersburg PA
CBHW020157200326
41521CB00006B/407